Praise for *Alchemy of Re...*

"The story of the cosmic integration of a soul frac... sexual abuse and troubled and suicidal mother who went on to re-create the puzzle of herself, piece by piece. Propelled by an indomitable spirit and an inner will to raise herself up from the morass of her human condition—supported by an equine companion who had likewise been abused—and powered by her conscious tie to God, she erected pillars of professional pursuits. Hertha then rebuilt her core identity until she could slowly allow the protective, defensive structure of a steeled persona to dissolve. Her momentum in this work became a force that morphed until all parts now have merged into that unity of oneness of a puzzle completed!"

—Lucille Sharp Yaney, LCSW and founder of the Inn of the Seventh Ray, Topanga, California

"I've always said no one knows what happens when we close our doors at night. Hertha has left her door ajar, and we can view her journey as an incredible example that, with God's help, everything is possible. *Alchemy of Resilience* reminded me that we are all given gifts by God. We must find them and use them to better ourselves and humanity. Hertha's gifts are many. It seems to me, she developed and used them all. Also, I believe that horses were given to Hertha, not only to ride but also to provide a vehicle to kindness, compassion, forgiveness, determination, and *love*."

—John Patterson, rancher, Columbus, Montana

"Hertha's book encapsulates a rancher's mentality. Her book captures the vast view of the country she witnessed from horseback at a young age. The tenacity, self-reliance, the ability to suck it up and keep on going no matter what, are all attributes she gained from her childhood on the ranch. My spiritual path has led me to know that sometimes those who God loves most are the ones who seem to suffer the most. I am grateful that Hertha opened the door to her heart and shared her experiences. My life is better for knowing her and reading her book."

—Jim Steinbeisser, past president of the Montana Stockgrowers and rancher, Sidney, Montana

"I feel very honored to be a part of Hertha's vital, beginning journey of healing. I cannot be more proud of what she has done with her life, who she is, and how she continues to help heal others through her beautiful work on herself and with her horses. *Alchemy of Resilience* is a very powerful, vulnerable, and profound book. It is very detailed, and the reader gets to feel the incredible psychological and emotional journey with her. Also, the reader can glean insights on what helped Hertha—her faith, strength, tenacity, and her love and trust for animals, as well as the horses along the way that helped guide her. *Alchemy of Resilience* will be incredibly transformative and illuminating to anyone who has the courage to read it and traverse their own journey simultaneously."
—Donna Lidren, PhD, Seattle, Washington

"What a beautiful and visceral experience Hertha put into form. She captured the cycle of her life that wanted and needed to complete. She tracked her process and offered her vulnerability to be witnessed through her story. To have witnessed her journey, through her darkest places, and to see her move through her shadow to find her light has been humbling. Hertha has added much to the collective integration and healing by sharing her personal journey. *Alchemy of Resilience* is truly an inspiration of dedication, loyalty, and to finding unconditional love. She walked, rode, and even swam through all the layers that she needed to. Finding her worthiness in her wholeness in the end is the greatest gift of all. It is my belief, '"We can't heal by ourselves. We are all one big herd after all."'
—Heidi Soper, body-mind-soul practitioner, Bozeman, Montana

Alchemy of Resilience

Alchemy of Resilience

My Rugged Path to Wholeness

HERTHA LUND

Revolution for Wholeness Publications
BOZEMAN, MONTANA, USA

Revolution for Wholeness Publications
Bozeman, Montana, USA
Copyright © 2023 by Hertha Lund. All rights reserved.

All rights reserved. No part of this publication may be reproduced, stored in a retrieval system or transmitted in any form or by any means (electronic, mechanical, photocopying, recording, or otherwise) without the written permission of the author and publisher.

Library of Congress Control Number: 2023911973
Paperback ISBN: 979-8-9885089-0-8
eBook ISBN: 979-8-9885089-1-5

Cover photo reprinted with permission by Phyllis Burchett
Author photo reprinted with permission by Fredrik Kalstveit

Book cover and interior design by Christina Thiele
Editorial production by kn literary

This book is dedicated to you, the reader. My deepest hope in writing this book and sharing my innermost experiences is that by reading it, your inner path to wholeness will be infused with courage and determination. I pray that my teaching by the example of my life will spark your will to embark on climbing the highest mountain to the summit of your divine being.

Contents

Foreword by Melisa Pearce ... 1
Introduction ... 3

PART I

Chapter 1: My Childhood: Heaven with Horses and Hell on Earth ... 9
Chapter 2: Golden Eagle ... 25
Chapter 3: Unresolved Pain ... 37
Chapter 4: Spiritual Mother ... 47
Chapter 5: Success and Starving ... 63
Chapter 6: Powering through Pain ... 79
Chapter 7: Dying to Live ... 97

PART II

Chapter 8: Heal Thyself ... 107
Chapter 9: Being Fully Present ... 121
Chapter 10: Compassion Is Key ... 135
Chapter 11: Integration and Embodiment on the Path ... 143
Chapter 12: Healing My Heart with Horses ... 157
Chapter 13: Keep Moving ... 167
Chapter 14: Who I Think I Am Matters ... 183
Chapter 15: Being Me Now ... 195

Epilogue ... 207
My Prayer ... 211
Acknowledgments ... 214
Endnotes ... 215
About the Author ... 217
About Four Horses for Wholeness ... 218

Foreword

Some memoirs inspire the reader to reach for more in life. Some memoirs touch the heart of the reader and elicit profound feelings. Some allow the reader to explore the similarity or contrast to their own lives. Some teach lessons to apply to our own lives. *Alchemy of Resilience offers it all to the reader.*

I am honored to have known Hertha Lund for several years as her mentor, educator, and therapist in her personal process to healing. I was her teacher in the Touched By A Horse training she pursued to become an Equine Gestalt Coach. I am moved by the authenticity of her writing as she takes us along with her on a very unusual and often painful journey.

Hertha's clear voice is heard throughout the book, as she journeys through her unique childhood, raised on a Montana ranch with a pony as her best friend. Hertha shares with the reader her life experiences with the many horses who provided solace, friendship, protection, and partnership throughout her life.

While some paths in our lives gently fork and we select the most appealing track forward, other paths come to a sudden and unforeseen end, forcing a distinct right or left turn. In this story, the reader is totally engaged with the twists, flow, and abrupt unanticipated turns due to Hertha's ability to express her experiences clearly and succinctly.

Her educational and professional path from a one-room schoolhouse on the prairie of Montana to obtaining her degree in journalism, and later becoming an attorney who served as a chief justice's first choice of a law clerk in Washington, DC, is a fascinating climb that illustrates to the reader what it takes to excel against all odds.

Today I respect Hertha as a competent professional peer. As an equine Gestaltist, Hertha works with clients who have experienced trauma. In the setting of her Montana ranch, she and her husband, John, host retreats and sessions for people to fully unplug and heal. On their Grande Ranch in Montana, along with cattle, she has her own beautiful Gypsy Vanner horses, a breed she first experienced in my barn.

Her courage is contagious. And this book allows the reader to reflect on the fluid flow we refer to as life. Hertha has taken stock of her life, and anyone who encounters her story will witness, through her eyes, a true journey to wholeness.

Profound questions for the "self" emerge as we read this book. The author's thinking and logic, combined with a deeply spiritual nature and connection to the divine, challenge us to ask deeper questions of ourselves.

The honest and clean way of expressing all Hertha has experienced, endured, and excelled in makes reading her story a wonderfully rich inner exploration for the reader of what it takes to truly heal.

—Melisa Pearce, creator of Equine Gestalt Coaching Method.
Melisa Pearce is a teacher, author, psychotherapist, and pioneer in the field of human/horse healing. Over the last three decades, she has coached and helped many others through her private psychotherapy practice and partnership with horses.

Introduction

"To know all things, including the painful and difficult, are lit from within by undivided light."

—Aura Glaser

Finally, after sixty years of this life, I feel free to be me. I feel more whole than I thought was ever possible. Each passing day, I experience life differently and now occupy my body fully with my divine geometry. I no longer feel alone and separate from all life around me. After passing through the portal of deep pain, I now feel deep gratitude to God and for every person in my life, especially those who instigated my reactions of pain, sadness, grief, and other feelings that I wanted to avoid. I now know that I need them.

My path in this life started with early childhood trauma due to my mom's volatility as well as sexual abuse starting at the age of five from the neighbor's teenage son. Looking back, I now know that even though some of my mom's abuse was physical and the teenage boy's abuse seemed to be all physical, the damage was more to my inner being and soul than my body. My body healed, but it remembered the trauma and the pain. Several years ago, as an adult, I spoke with the now-grown man who had abused me those many years ago, and I now believe that he did not intend to cause the damage that he left inside me at spiritual and emotional levels of being. I also know that regardless of his intentions, his actions left me with deep feelings of unworthiness to receive love, including from God. Since I was a little girl and did not know any better, I took into my body the shame that really belonged to him. Through the journey described in this book, his shame is no longer part of me.

During my Gestalt training, often at the end of a process in which my classmates have portrayed a person in my life, I consciously de-role that person in my mind. At this stage in my life, I de-role each person who hurt me, including my mom, then the boy who abused me, the children who were mean to me because I was white and the ones who were mean because they thought I was Native American, and the leaders in church and state who rejected me. I imagine some of what each of these people did was "wrong" because it hurt me at multiple levels of being. I also imagine that once I heal from the hurt, the person who used their free will to hurt another life will carry a greater burden from their hurtful actions than I have. There is no amount of "wrong" that cannot be forgiven. So, I ask for divine forgiveness and a great amount of love to be poured into and upon each and every soul that has harmed me. I desire to see all life reunited with wholeness.

I now know from within that we are all one. My path toward wholeness used my pain to move forward. My new consciousness of embodied soul freedom is still very much in its infancy stage. I am grateful for the opportunity to climb the mountain of wholeness.

INTRODUCTION

Life Is a Treasure Hunt for Inner Mysteries

Life is like a treasure hunt
As I travel to and fro, I unveil my own inner mysteries
I walk down paths that are virgin territory to my moccasins
I climb mountains that have always seemed impassable from a distance
My toes always point in one direction—forward
As I keep moving forward, down this trail and up this path
I discover flowers along the way whose fragrance and beauty would have escaped my senses
If I hadn't walked into the forest
Now this treasure hunting must be done alone
For the chatter of well-meaning friends can mean that a flower remains veiled in the dense underbrush
One doesn't want to backtrack to catch what one missed the first time around
And, of course, flowers do not stand in full bloom forever
The flower could be wilted by the time one comes back to uncover it
Now, there is still beauty, it is just that the fragrance isn't as refreshing
The petals aren't as magnificent
The experience isn't as enthralling
Truly, one must take advantage of these beautiful flowers when the treasure is first offered
The beauty of one treasure adds to another until one has a vast chest full of treasures
of unveiled inner mysteries

Part I

CHAPTER 1

My Childhood: Heaven with Horses and Hell on Earth

∞

I feel lonely
I feel like a little girl abandoned deep in the ocean
I feel little, elusive, shy, and hungry
I feel lonely

I feel rejected
I feel like a little girl sitting on the curb alone
I feel caved in, unworthy, and alone
I feel rejected

I feel angry
I feel like a little girl banged against the rocks
I feel bloody, battered, black and blue, and beat up
I feel angry

I feel sad
I feel like a forgotten, abused little puppy
I am wet, crying, little, spotted, and alone
I feel sad

I feel scared
I have no home
I feel like a bird with no nest
I feel tired of flapping my wings
I feel scared because maybe nobody cares

I feel angry
I have been tricked
I feel like a foolish fish
I took the bait
When I swallowed the hook
She reeled and threw me out of the boat
I feel angry

MY CHILDHOOD: HEAVEN WITH HORSES AND HELL ON EARTH

I feel hurt
I feel like a zebra in a herd of horses
I feel I do not belong
I feel bad, black and blue, battered, kicked, and bitten
I feel hurt

I feel like quitting, that scares me

My parents, Jeanne and Robert Lund, lived near Zortman, Montana, on a ranch that was made up of very little private land and many acres of rugged breaks in an area managed by the Bureau of Land Management. The closest town was Malta, which was forty-eight miles away. My older brother, Ron, survived being born there three years prior to my birth. But John Robert had not survived due to his birth defects. My mom grieved the loss of John Robert, and she could not bear going back to Malta to deliver what she thought was her next child. Not knowing she was pregnant with twins, my mom scheduled a date to deliver at a hospital further away.

My mom chose to travel to Great Falls, which was 120 miles from home. She was thirty-six years old when she showed up for her scheduled delivery of a baby on May 29, 1962. A student nurse there told my mom that she thought she heard two heartbeats. As my mom told the story, the doctor chastised the nurse for saying such a thing and potentially scaring my mom at the thought of having twins.

After delivering my brother Harlan, the doctor started to leave the delivery room, and as the story goes, a nurse said, "You better get back over here. There is another baby coming feet first." The doctor pulled me into the world, and Harlan and I were put into incubators because we were both around four pounds. So, I began life as an afterthought, deprived of the arms of a loving mom and instead given the incubator and a stranger's touch. My mom's giving birth to twins unexpectedly at age thirty-six made the newspaper, in part because my grandfather

George Lund was attending a board of regents meeting with my mom's doctor, who had to leave the meeting early to attend to our birth.

My mom told me that having twins to care for was quite hard because she loved working on the ranch. My recollection is that she was not really maternal material. She hired women to help her take care of the house and her children. Mom loved being outside in nature, working or fishing or hunting, and she could fix almost anything, from the roof to a vehicle. One of her geniuses was her ability to create and fix things from the resources she had around her—she could create a new toy scabbard from old boot leather. Her mind worked overtime and kept her awake at night until she figured out how to fix or create whatever she was working on. She had very little patience for anything she could not fix and control, including me. (It appears I inherited this trait because, for much of my life, I desired to fix my mom.)

My memories of my childhood do not truly start until the time I was around four years old. I remember a few things and feelings of being horrendously sad or terrified. We lived in an old wood cabin with chinking between the logs and an attached small trailer house. It was a very simple structure that barely took up space on the vast landscape created by the Missouri River breaks. I remember trying to get away from the house whenever I could. At four, I started riding horses, and this allowed me to escape being near my mom.

Ranching families typically acquire a very gentle horse and then have other horses that children can graduate to as they develop the ability to safely handle and ride horses. Twins disrupt this natural order because a family does not typically have two very gentle horses. I was more of a go-getter than Harlan, so I started riding first. Big Black was the name of our horse—he was more than twenty and a pony cross of some type. But he was much larger than most ponies and a very kind, gentle horse with gray and speckled white hair mixed into his black coat. Big Black was the perfect kids' horse. He would walk out and turn and was very patient and kind to those of us who learned to ride on him. But my time with Big Black was short because I needed to move on so Harlan could start riding.

My mom taught us—with much intensity—to never tie a horse up to something unsolid. She had lost her favorite horse because Ron tied it to his rocking horse, and the horse dragged it for quite some ways. Then, my dad made her get rid of that beloved horse because he was scared of what might happen if one of us kids got caught in something attached to the horse. Both Mom and Dad told us again and again to never tie anything to the horses. Even with these repeated warnings, my brothers, who were partners in shenanigans on the ranch, talked me into riding Big Black while they rode in the red toy wagon that they tied to Big Black with ropes from the tongue of the wagon.

Big Black did not run off with the wagon with me on top of him bareback. Something much worse happened. My mom saw what we were doing and came on the rampage. Ron and Harlan, who had been sitting in the wagon, ran away. I was stuck on top of Big Black with all the ropes between him and the wagon dragging behind us. I was not afraid of Big Black. He stood solid and was very careful to not hurt me. My mom was not so solid or careful. I was afraid of her and her emotional tirades.

She had her own unresolved childhood sexual abuse trauma that seemed to be triggered by my birth—I was the oldest daughter in our family. Also, her mother's mother abandoned her family and left my grandma to raise her siblings. So, my arrival probably triggered some memory of her mom's unresolved mother wounds. In those days there were few resources for women living in rural Montana more than forty miles from any area with healthcare services, which likely would not have included mental health services anyway. Instead of seeking assistance, my mom drank whiskey and beer and worked hard on the ranch to numb her inner pain.

Since much of my trauma from my mom occurred before the age of four, I do not have many memories of all that happened. Also, since these deep wounds happened before I could talk, it is hard for me to find words to describe what happened and how I felt. Now, I am aware that to survive I did my best to not feel, which also makes it very hard to share what I do remember.

I remember that when I was in first grade and could not find my shoes one morning, my mom wrapped her hands around my neck, picked me up off the ground, and choked me. I clearly remember my awareness, as she held me eye to eye, that I had a mom who could kill me. She seemed shocked and dropped and abandoned me in the room. I did not struggle and I did not cry out, for at that early age, I already knew that anything less than seeming surrender when I was in her hands would potentially lead to greater harm or fulfill my terror of her killing me. Also, I remember feeling totally confused, vulnerable, and absolutely frightened of my mom. There must have been times when she loved me, for I did feel love. However, I was predominantly terrified of being anywhere close to her because I never knew which mom would show up. And so, I left the house early in the morning and played outside until I had to come back in to find food or because of the weather.

After I graduated from riding Big Black, I had my first very own horse, Little Red. He was a pretty blood bay Shetland pony and was very green-broke, which meant he had just started getting used to me riding him bareback. I fell in love with Little Red despite his many shortcomings. When I escaped with Little Red from my mom and my house, I felt free and safe on the vast, rough, sagebrush-covered ground surrounding our house. Riding him was my portal to another world. I felt connected with another being and transported to conversations with God. Being with Little Red outside with Mother Nature and talking to Spirit gave me hope that my life was not limited to my soul-wrenching experiences with my mom. I can never remember a time that I was not terrified that my mom would hurt herself, me, or someone else.

To escape these feelings, I rode Little Red bareback and pretended I was a Native American scout. I would ride him to the far end of the several-acre pasture that surrounded our ranch buildings, and he would shy—move sideways with speed—and I would fall off in the sagebrush and cactus. He would then run off, and I would cry because Little Red had abandoned me and because of the physical wounds of being dumped in the rough terrain. My wounds were usually scraped knees and elbows, sometimes a bloody nose, and bruises from where I hit the ground. The walk back home to catch up with Little Red took me at least half an hour, during which time I would usually get angry at my pony. Even though I would get angry, as soon as I saw Little Red, my heart melted, and I immediately forgave him. He let me catch him, and we would begin our adventures again. I did not share the danger of my days with Little Red with my parents because I did not want them to take away my freedom to play with him.

Even though my adventures with Little Red were somewhat risky, to me it seemed much less risky than staying in the house where mom might interact with me or hanging out with my brothers, who didn't always act with my safety in mind. I remember when Harlan and I received bicycles for our fifth birthdays. Soon after, I mastered riding the bike without training wheels—I thought they were stupid. Ron's birthday was several months after ours, and he received a mini motorbike that year. Ron and Harlan spent a lot of time trying to convince me that it would be a good idea for them to tie my bicycle behind the mini-bike and pull me down the gravel road. I conceded. Harlan and Ron were in front of me on the mini-bike, the rope went tight, and soon I was moving so fast that I could no longer pedal. I picked my feet up and just held them out of the way of the whirring pedals. For a moment, I thought the speed was exciting and fun. Also, I felt like I was no longer an outsider from the bond between my brothers. Then the corner came, my hind tire slid on the loose gravel, and the bike and I were dragged across the road until I came loose. I cried all the way back to the house. Before I could open the door, my mom came out in a fit of anger because I was covered in scrapes and blood from head to toe. She demanded to know what happened to me. I was so scared of her reaction that I had a hard time explaining through my tears my brothers' scheme of tying my bike behind the mini-bike. I never expected support, comfort, or protection. Also, I did not want to get my brothers in trouble—I feared for them.

Somehow, I survived my older brothers' capers, my mom's lack of maternal instincts, and running wild through the sagebrush and rough country in the Missouri River breaks. Even though the landscape was understated colors of mostly muted grays, browns, and sometimes a little green, the natural beauty infused life into my soul. I loved the vast openness. Also, I could look forever and see nothing but more rough country. Spending time alone as a child in this landscape helped me to be comfortable within myself. The country is so immense, open, and rugged that to feel anything less than secure within oneself could lead to a terror of insignificance on the face of the earth. Instead of feeling fear when I was out in nature with my horses, I felt like I belonged and was nurtured in the folds of the earth. It was my happy place—my home.

Since I was horse-crazy, the small, old wood barn was my favorite place on our ranch. We also had a milk cow, and when the man who worked for us on the ranch milked her, he would squirt milk across the stall into the cats' mouths. I loved watching this. I loved the dusty, warm, cozy smells of hay that permeated the barn. The horses ate their treats and oats in there, and it felt like a sacred place apart from the harsh world outside the barn's door.

Even though the horse barn was my favorite place, it was also home to one of my worst childhood experiences. A neighbor teenage boy sexually abused me there. I did what he told me because he had already abused me at his house multiple times. He threatened to hurt me or my family to keep me from telling my parents or his about what he had done to me. He also bribed me with promises of rides on his motorcycle.

I never told my parents about his abuse for several reasons. I felt ashamed and dirty and that it was my fault. Also, my mom had told me that she would kill anybody that harmed her children—and I believed her. I did not want her to kill someone and go to jail. Even though I was only five, I decided I needed to protect my mom instead of trusting her to protect me in a loving manner.

Even though I was daddy's girl, I never told him about the sexual abuse, either. He was always very busy working on and managing the ranch. He called me Hershey Babe, and I loved him. But I did not feel like I could tell him about what the neighbor boy did to me. I did not feel like I should trouble him since he was hardly around. Also, I felt I would let him down. And I knew that if my dad knew about the neighbor boy's hurting me that meant Mom would know too. I did not believe my dad could keep my mom from killing the neighbor boy. So, I never told anybody, and my experience and my pain, shame, guilt, sense of unworthiness, and terror was stuffed inside me—I had no support.

I sought solace with the horses and in nature. I wanted to feel safe and loved, but I did not trust my mom, so I didn't feel safe in my home. I felt safe when I was playing with my horses and talking to God in the vast, rough country surrounding our home. This is when I first shared the burdens of my heart with my horse. I felt heard, seen, and loved. We had several mares who had colts every year, and I observed them and how they quietly nickered to their foals. I pretended I was a colt, too, and that the mares were also loving me with the gentle movements and soft noises they shared with their baby horses.

One of the mares was named Susie. I was allowed to graduate from Little Red to Susie for ranch work when she was not being a mom to her foals. I was barely five when I talked dad into letting me ride on the all-day gathers of cows. We herded the cattle in from the rugged, deep gullies carved into the vast landscape that we called "the breaks." The breaks were covered with purple-gray sagebrush that grew tall enough to almost touch Susie's belly. When she walked through the sagebrush, I caught the plant's dusty, poignant fragrance. I could see for miles and watch clouds on the horizon as I rode. As Susie and I walked along, I felt like I was one with the great universe of God and that I could see it all from her back.

My dad, the hired men who worked for him, my older brother, Ron, and I would saddle up the horses to leave the barn at, or right before, sunrise. Sometimes we did not return until late in the afternoon. Dad made me promise not to cry or cause trouble during the long day of riding miles from our home. I discovered that I could sleep and stay on top of Susie as she followed the other horses. I thought I was in heaven to be outside all day with my horse.

My little sister was born when I was three. I have very little memory of her as a baby because Mom sent Heidi to the hired man's wife to take care of her. Maybe Mom had learned with me that she was not safe with girl babies. Mom seemed to be different with my brothers. In my recollection, boy children were the ones who were going to carry forward the family ranch. Even though my mom was handier than my dad with tools, heavy machinery, animal husbandry, and many other physical aspects of ranching, our family was no different from most others regarding the boys being destined to inherit the ranch. Ron and Harlan had a different childhood than either Heidi or me.

Sometimes, Mom was extremely fun to be around. She would sing silly songs while she was driving us to places near the Missouri River where we would have a picnic, play, fish, and watch the bighorn sheep fight on the steep cliff on the other side of the river. Mom spent many hours making things like a scabbard for my brothers' hunting knives out of an old pair of ranch boots, or other ingenious creations that we could use to assist us in ranch life. I loved it when she showed up as her fun-loving, creative self. Yet, I never knew for sure when she might shift to the darker side of her personality.

MY CHILDHOOD: HEAVEN WITH HORSES AND HELL ON EARTH

When we lived near Zortman and the Little Rocky Mountains, my two brothers and I attended a one-room schoolhouse with six other kids, whose ages lined up with ours. The school did not have running water, and we had to trudge to the outhouse for bathroom breaks. During recess, we played rural kids' games such as fox and goose, red rover, and football. I remember loving my time at school. One recess we caught a baby rabbit from underneath the cattle guard that was in front of the school. The rabbit shrieked in fear when we touched it—a piercing sound that I would never forget. We were gentle with the baby and let it go, even though we wanted to keep it as a pet.

During second grade my family moved from Zortman to Browning, Montana. My mom and dad bought land on the Blackfeet Reservation, and as non-Native Americans, we joined a minority in the population. The change from a rural, one-room schoolhouse with my eight classmates, all from three neighboring families, to being in a classroom with thirty classmates was hard for me to cope with. Early on, one of my classmates asked me if I was Indian. I had lots of dark hair and a dusky complexion, so I looked as—or more—indigenous than many others in my class. I was brought up to tell the truth, so I answered that I was not. I had no idea that my response would be so heartbreaking for me.

I was articulate and a bit of a smart aleck, which unfortunately enhanced my status as a target for bullying by the students who picked on those who were not of Native American descent. At one point, an older and much bigger girl was telling me off and saying how disgusting I was. Instead of minding my tongue, I talked back to her. She responded, "Piss on you." I retorted that she was not tall enough. She got mad and chased me in an attempt to beat me. I was pretty athletic and an extreme tomboy, and my fear was greater than her anger, so I outran her.

But I was not able to outrun all those who wanted to chase me down and hit me. One day during recess, a group of eight or more girls cornered and caught me. I had taken my football back from a boy in my class who had stolen it from me. He told this group of girls, who turned into a mob and surrounded me. Then they fought among themselves to determine who would get to hit me with their fists. I stayed still as they were fighting around me because I sensed that, like a pack of wolves, if I moved, they would pounce on me.

Finally, they declared a winner, and the girl who won the right to pummel me stepped forward. I felt scared, but I did not let them know. I was determined not to let them see me cry, so I just stood there with my hands down. But since I was not fighting back, the girl who had won the right to hit me had a hard time. She wound up to slug me in the face and ended up hitting me with a glancing blow that slid off my cheek instead of squarely. The girls who had surrounded me in a circle to keep me from getting away laughed at their friend for missing a standing target. This of course made her angrier, and she hit me again. All of a sudden, they all left me standing there by myself. When they were out of range to see or hear me, I cried and cried. I felt I belonged nowhere among people.

In an attempt to fit in, I helped my fellow students with their schoolwork. Sometimes I even went against what my parents had taught me and helped them cheat to pass the school tests. I did my best to not display my ability to read and do classwork above my grade level. I did not want to stand out; I just wanted to fit in and have friends.

Growing up on our ranch with my brothers, along with my natural tomboy inclinations, helped me to excel in sports. I often played tackle football with the boys because they were not as mean as the girls. Even though I was the only girl, I was often picked high up in the selection process because I was tough, could tackle effectively, and worked very hard even though it was just a game during school recess.

I was physically tough, but super sensitive emotionally. At a spiritual level, I was unable to understand why people would fight among themselves to determine who would win the opportunity to hurt me. I felt gutted and heartbroken by my experience of the cruelty of life.

Not all my life experiences were bad during the time my family lived on the reservation. Our ranch covered thirty thousand acres of some of the most beautiful rolling grasslands in America. In the distance, I could see the Rocky Mountains, with Chief Mountain being a sentinel overlooking our ranch. During the summer, I went native and spent every waking moment outside. Much of the time, I was on horseback. Sometimes we would start riding before sunup and not return from the day's work until dinnertime. I had found my bliss, spending all day horseback riding through the cows on the beautiful landscape near the Milk River that flowed through the northernmost part of our ranch.

Riding horseback was not always heaven. One time, I was sitting in the shade in front of Susie, and she struck at a fly and pawed me in the back of my head. Dick, our hired man who I often rode with, was scared that I might have a concussion. It was more than ninety degrees out, and we were hours away from any transportation other than the horses. I had a ferocious headache and felt sick to my stomach. But I made it home that day—and probably was ready to ride again the next day.

The other part of riding horses all day that was not heaven was that sometimes Dick would tell me dirty jokes or stories. I did not really like him telling me dirty jokes, even though I was clever with words and wanted to fit in—but it seemed like something was not right. Dick and his wife lived at the far north end of our ranch in buildings we called Buck Place, which was less than thirty miles from the Canadian border. Buck Place was also more than thirty miles from the main part of our ranch where my mom was running large haying equipment for part of the summer months. Sometimes I stayed with Dick and his wife to help ride and care for the livestock, which was also a means for me to get far away from my mom and for her to get us out of her way. Also, my sister Heidi stayed there often, so I was able to spend time with her.

Escaping to Buck Place was a very mixed experience for me. I loved the expansive grasslands and riding near the Milk River where I could see forever and ride for hours without seeing anyone besides Dick. However, Dick also took liberties to touch me between my legs when he helped me get on my horse. I was too small to get on a tall horse by myself. I was only eight or nine. I remember telling him that I did not like it when he touched me, but I also remember feeling very conflicted—if I made him mad, I could not escape my mom and ride in my paradise.

Working on the ranch and riding horses on the vast, rolling grasslands with the Rocky Mountains in sight, I learned a lot from Mother Nature. One time, I was out walking in the horse pasture and came upon a huge ant hill that was three feet around and elevated at least one foot above the surrounding ground. I stopped and viewed the ants all scurrying about that ant hill. It dawned on me that the ants did not know I was looking down and observing them. They did not know about my world and our home ranch thirty miles away. I realized that my perspective was probably similar to that of God or the angels who might be watching down upon me as I scurried about in my limited world.

Another lesson I learned while living on that ranch is that no matter how bad the moment or the weather seems, it will change. I loved helping to bring cattle into the corrals from vast areas of the ranch, except sometimes during the fall gather when it would be late enough in the year that we would get cold weather and blizzards. A blizzard on the Rocky Mountain Front can be and usually is a very serious, dangerous event.

I remember a time it was snowing so hard, I could not see my horse's ears while I was sitting on top of him. I cried because I was scared and felt like my feet were going to freeze. There was no one around me, so it was up to me and my horse to make it home safely. I gave my horse his head, and we followed the cows into the corrals less than an hour later. As I was trusting my horse to know the way home in the blizzard, I told myself over and over that even though I was very uncomfortable because of the cold and my fears for survival, I would soon be home, warming up by the stove and drinking hot chocolate. In addition to having awareness of the changing weather, I also learned, in that moment, to be able to stay calm and withstand bouts of bad weather and trust my horse to get me home safely. I believe that day with my horse in the storm planted the seeds for resilience and the ability to handle many of my future life challenges.

∞

CHAPTER 2

Golden Eagle

∞

I shall run no longer
No longer shall I fight my destination
Though my moccasins have traveled many trails
There is only one true path
This path is the one leading to the Great Spirit

The Earth is my Mother
The Great Spirit my Father
From this moment on I thrust the arrow of life toward the heavens
No longer shall I tarry
I will pursue and endure this path

When my moccasins become worn, I shall step forward barefoot
When my feet bleed, I shall rejoice
For I know the trail is not well-traveled or smooth
The rocks that prick my feet are obstacles to overcome in becoming who I am

I thank all the heavens for the gift of your presence in my life
I love you very much
I know not what the future will bring or where the path will lead me
I do know that wherever I am, I have special love and prayer in my heart for you

After living the first six years of my life in the Missouri River breaks, and then living on the Blackfeet Reservation for the next six and half years, my family sold the ranch on the reservation and bought a smaller ranch near Lewistown in the geographical center of Montana. This is the first time my mom and dad had a ranch that was all privately owned land instead of ranching on leased land. When we lived in the Missouri River breaks, much of our ranch was on land managed by the Bureau of Land Management. Similarly, when we ranched near Browning, our ranch had substantial leased portions from the Blackfeet Tribe.

It was 1975 when we moved to Lewistown, and I was in seventh grade—junior high. The adjustment to a new school and new town was hard for me—I did not fit in for several reasons. One reason was that after being bullied and feeling like an outsider for much of my time on the reservation (for being a "white woman") I now suffered being called "squaw." I had grown my hair out down to my waist and often wore it in two thick braids. With my dark complexion and dark hair, I looked like I was of Native American descent. Sometimes when I went into stores, those who worked in the store would follow me to see if was going to steal something, displaying their prejudice. I would get so ornery that if I caught them following me, I would lead them on a wild goose chase, walking up and down the aisles, acting shifty and nervous like I was getting ready to swipe something.

When we moved to Lewistown, it seemed like my mom's drinking got worse. Maybe it didn't, or maybe at the age of thirteen, I was old enough to notice more of what was going on around me. At any rate, when we lived in Browning my mom would drink at least one half to one full fifth of whiskey per day. She also drank beer continuously. Mom drank so much that my sister, up until adulthood, didn't comprehend that a person could get drunk from drinking beer. Mom could drink two six-packs, and she would just seem a bit more outgoing and sentimental. She certainly did not seem drunk to us. But once we all lived in the smaller house on the smaller ranch and did not have all the land to spread out on that we had in Browning, the dysfunction in our family became more apparent.

We had fewer acres and seven of us were living in a five-bedroom house, so I found it harder to avoid my mom for days at a time like I had when we lived on the reservation. Also, at thirteen I felt emotions other than terror from being around my mom. I remember feeling self-conscious because I realized that my mom was not like my friends' mothers. My mom did not like to do anything social unless she was well-lubricated. Then, in that state, she was unpredictable, and I never knew who would show up. Sometimes she was funny and entertaining. Sometimes she was lewd and scary. Sometimes she was morose and foreboding and threatened suicide.

When my mom was in her suicidal phase and would go missing, my heart raced and I felt nauseous. I felt terror to the core of my being and in every cell of my body. I could not let her abandon me and my siblings. I had to keep her alive, so I decided that it was my job to take care of her. When she was missing, I would go look for her on our ranch. More than once, I found her with her rifle across her knees, a beer in her hand, and a glossy look in her eyes. I would approach her and tell her, "Mom, I love you. This is not you." My belief was that if I loved her enough, my love would pull her through the clutches of the demon far enough that she would decide not to kill herself. Tears streamed down my face as I boldly loved her with a vulnerability that I summoned because I wanted to bypass the darkness and reach her heart. She would look at me, and every time she seemed to recognize that she was breaking my heart. Somehow, she would pull herself together, promise me she was not going to kill herself, and ask me to leave her while she finished pulling herself back together.

After many of these experiences of excruciating pain and expressing love to save my mom, I again found surcease and comfort with my horses. When I buried my face in my mare Lisa's furry neck, I let my tears go, and she stood with me as I felt so much pain and sadness I feared it would kill me. I felt Lisa supporting me as I collapsed on her neck. The horse barn was within walking distance of the house, and my sister and I spent a lot of time there feeding and caring for the horses. It was our home away from home.

When we lived near Browning, I had competed in a few rodeos. My parents bought me my first barrel racing horse, John, who was fifteen or sixteen and very seasoned at the sport. I was only nine years old when I first got him and pretty small. John and I would enter the youth and the ladies' barrel racing at the local rodeos. We did well together and often won money.

After the move, I did not have as much ranch work to call me away from the house and my mom, so I really focused on my rodeo skills. I learned how to rope and how to jump off my horse to catch and tie a ribbon on the tail of a goat. At this point, John became my main horse for roping and all the events besides barrel racing. My parents had also bought Lisa, who was a speed demon, so I ran barrels on her. I loved Lisa because she was bold, beautiful, and did not give in to anyone. She had the horrible habit of always wanting to go at least one level of speed faster than her rider wanted her to go. Her riders would battle her when we wanted her to walk, and she would push against the bit and try to go faster to trot. Finally, I learned that if I pulled on the reins and showed her the speed I wanted her to go rather than try to contain her with the reins, she would then do a fast walk without pushing against the bit. She taught me that using force would never contain her spirit.

I remember one day when my twin brother saddled Lisa to go move cows on the meadow where I had been training her for upcoming match races. I would match race her against proven racehorses during our summer horse show and 4-H fair. Lisa did not respond to Harlan's attempts to contain her. He came back to the house spitting mad. He asked me if I had been training Lisa in the pasture where he went to gather cows. I replied that I had. He told me that when he got there, she just took off, running as fast as she could instead of obeying him to work the cows. To train her and get her in shape, I breezed her—I let her run as fast as she could on the meadow. It was flat and did not have gopher holes for her to fall and break a leg like many pastures do. Running Lisa flat out as fast as she could go made my eyes water and was thrilling. Based on Harlan's response, he did not appreciate Lisa's speed in the same way.

In addition to loving Lisa's speed, I also loved developing the skills I needed to excel in rodeo events. I was very disciplined, and I practiced often in our makeshift arena where we had plowed some ground in a field next to the house. Sometimes, I practiced in the hot sun until I had sunstroke. My drive to win was all-consuming. My goal was not just to be better than others. Instead, I used my love of horses and learning rodeo events to channel my drive to excel individually, which, paired with my goal to escape my house and my problems with my mom, meant I won many buckles and one saddle before I entered high school.

My other escape was drinking with my brothers and their friends. Ron was three years ahead of Harlan and me in school. Ron and Harlan were always together, so Ron often ended up taking me along on their excursions, allowing all of us to get out of the house. We had all started drinking hard liquor at around the age of twelve when we lived on the reservation. We had been considered goody-goodies back there because many of our friends were smoking cigarettes and doing whatever drugs were available at that time, and we only drank Black Velvet straight. Drinking beer with our new Lewistown friends was an easy transition.

Even though I started drinking alcohol early in my life, I was disciplined whenever I was involved in rodeo or playing sports and stopped drinking during those times. As a freshman, I made the junior varsity basketball team and worked hard to learn the game of basketball. The next year, I played varsity. I was strong with quick reflexes, but not really very fast. Also, I was simply not as athletically gifted as some of the other girls. But nobody outworked me either at practice or in a game. In my junior year, our team, the Fergus Golden Eagles, won third at state.

Even though I knew I was a leader on the team, I was not chosen to be captain of the basketball team during my senior year. There were four of us who had all played together for the previous three years, and the team chose the other two to be co-captains. I felt a little slighted and overlooked. Also, I had to play guard because our starting center was six-feet-three-inches tall, one of our forwards was six feet, and the other forward was five feet ten. At five feet nine, even though I had out-rebounded the three taller girls on our team at camp, it was up to me to learn how to play out of my natural inclination to be a forward and transition to playing guard. I used my brains and my quickness to play guard the best I could.

At the state tournament my senior year, we were in the championship game and ahead with nine minutes left. It seemed like our team had shifted into the twilight zone and quit playing. We were so close to the goal we had set for ourselves, and we just lost our focus. I looked at my teammates and decided it was up to me to spark their attention back into the game. The opposing team threw the ball so close to me that I tipped it, but I could not get control of it, and it went out of bounds. They did it again, and this time I stole the ball and dribbled all the way down the floor to our basket and made a layup. These two sparks of extra energy got my teammates back into the game, and we went on to win and cut down the nets. It was the first time in history that the Fergus Golden Eagles girls' basketball team won the state title.

Later, our center, who was one year behind me, told me that until after I was no longer on the team, she didn't realize all that I had brought to it. I was not the best shooter, the best dribbler, or the best at anything. I was pretty good at defense, and I left it all on the court. Most of all, by playing out of my natural position and understanding the talent around me, I learned how to put myself aside and focus on making others better. Winning a state championship together was not about me. It was about all of us working hard to create the relationships and skills to play well together as a team.

When I was not involved in basketball and rodeo seasons, I felt a little lost. Even though I had some good friends and a very sweet boyfriend for a couple of years, I still did not feel I fit in anywhere.

Sometimes, to cope, I drank too much. Other times, I buried myself in striving to get good grades in school, being a leader in the Future Farmers of America (FFA), being a leader in 4-H, and my athletic endeavors.

My mom and I often fought because we did not seem to see eye to eye on anything. When I was a sophomore, she asked me what I wanted for Christmas. She seemed earnest, and I told her from deep in my heart that for Christmas I wanted her to quit drinking. She cried, but she did not stop drinking. At this time, we were living in the house of her dreams. The ranch had been having money problems, and they sold the piece of property where the old house stood. They then bought this beautiful house on the hill to make mom happy. It did not work.

Dad was around six feet tall and pretty stocky in build. He had a square-shaped head and lots of hair. He always wore glasses and had one glass eye because he was hurt as a child doing something with a calf. In the ensuing surgery, the doctor mistakenly cut a nerve, so Dad could not hear out of one ear either. One time, when we traveled to go to a cousin's wedding, my dad drank too much. I went into his room to wake him up, and his false teeth and his eye were on the nightstand. I jokingly asked him if these body parts were having a conversation without him. He thought my quirky sense of humor was funny, and he valued that I read a lot and very fast from a young age. He was very intelligent and had graduated from high school at sixteen and gone to college to study mining engineering.

When my dad did not do anything to help my mom, I would feel very frustrated. I wanted him to help her so she wasn't so miserable. My dad would act like he was disgusted with my mom's inability to quit drinking and live a more positive life. He seemed to think that she had the power to decide whether or not she was an addict. He, like many others of his generation (born in 1925), did not develop the awareness or compassion to assist loved ones in dealing with and overcoming their inner demons.

My concern about my mom drove me to look inward as well as upward. I had an innate connection with God from a very early age. To me, asking God for help was not a learned response from religious training; instead, praying was a matter of survival. My mom would often drive while drinking and after consuming alcohol all day. She would be blasted while driving with us kids in the vehicle, pulling a loaded horse trailer. For some reason unknown to me, I was often with her alone during these scary times. Maybe my love for her and desire to save her caused me to separate myself from my brothers, who abandoned that ship and traveled with dad instead. They often drove separately to the rodeo, 4-H event, or whatever we attended with our horses because of my dad's work schedule—and because they did not get along. Also, our whole family would not fit in a pickup (there were only single-seaters at that time). Anyhow, I clearly remember asking God, from a feeling of terror, to keep our vehicle on the road and help us all get home safely. Knowing how drunk my mom was while she was driving, coupled with the dangers of the roads we were on, it is a miracle that we never crashed or had some type of incident.

Traveling to and from rodeos with my mom was a mixed experience. I loved traveling, competing, and being with my horse friends. I loved the inner challenge and goal setting required for me to develop the inner and outer skills to win. I loved seeing and connecting with the women who were my mentors in the rodeo arena. But my mom's unpredictability always had me on edge. She often used the excuse of being away from home and the social setting of the rodeo to drink more than her normal near-fifth of whisky per day. In a more lubricated condition, she often said and did embarrassing things. She sometimes threatened physical harm. She often got emotionally abusive toward me on the drive home. If I did not win, she would tell me that the only reason why was because I was trying to embarrass her. I remember how horrible it was to be stuck in the pickup with her berating me.

I just had to sit and take her tirades. At least by the time I was in high school, I could drive us. She would still be drinking, and she still took her inner battle out on me until she fell asleep. But with me behind the wheel, I was no longer under the terror of her wrecking our rig and killing us—and my horses.

During these long, hundred-mile drives, when I was trapped in the vehicle with my mom, I felt overwhelmed by multiple cascading emotions. I felt extreme emotional pain because I felt I could do nothing to please my mom. I felt terrified because when my mom was drunk, I never knew what she might do next. Part of me wanted to run away and never be near her again. But another part put up with the terror because my mother's desire to get out of the house to drink more freely at the rodeos was my ticket to pursue my passion to compete on horseback. I loved my time partnering with my horses in the practice pen and competing in the arena, and I loved setting goals and achieving them.

My dad was mostly missing in action. He sometimes showed up at the rodeo to watch the competitions. One time when I was in a position to win a state championship, something went wrong, and I did not come out on top. I was walking my horse in an area where there were no people and crying because I had tried so hard and failed to win first. My dad came walking up behind me and comforted me, something I saw little of in my childhood.

My sense is that he had no idea how bad Mom could be on these trips or the danger she put me and my siblings in with her drunk driving. But if he were not running from her and her problems, he could have figured it out. I longed for an adult to somehow help my mom deal with her pain because it was killing me slowly. I felt like a lobster being slowly boiled to death in my mom's pain.

Even though I was a daddy's girl and mostly felt loved and supported by him, there were other ways that he sometimes failed to support me. When Harlan and I were in high school, we were both nominated to be president of our school's chapter of FFA. I felt so excited, honored, and accepted that all the guys in my class might elect me to be their leader. When I got home and told my dad that both of us were nominated, he said, "Hertha, you will drop out." I stiffened up and told him that I would not withdraw and that Harlan would. I knew that Harlan did not want the extra work of being the president and that his shyness kept him from seeking leadership positions. This was the first time that I went against my dad. I realized that I had a drive inside of me to succeed that got lit up when somebody told me I could not follow my heart's passion. I was elected as the first girl president of the Fergus chapter of FFA.

∞

CHAPTER 3

Unresolved Pain

Even though I competed well enough to be a state champion in break-away roping and basketball during the same year of high school, I was also able to get good grades. When I was applying for college, my goal was to become a veterinarian. I wanted to be a horse doctor. Initially, I applied and was accepted to Colorado State University, and I was excited to get away from home. But for some reason I do not remember, I changed my plans and ended up attending Montana State University (MSU) in Bozeman, Montana.

Once I arrived at MSU, I decided to try out for the basketball team. I was one of many who tried out and one of four who were asked to join the team as a walk-on, or a player not on a scholarship. I played very hard and loved the challenge. My contribution ended up being hard competition for the starters in practice situations. Physically, I was very strong, my work ethic helped me develop into a good defensive player, and I was selfless. Also, during my first year of college, I competed in the college rodeos and made it to the College National Finals Rodeo. In addition to my sports and activities, I was studying pre-vet, pre-medicine, animal science, and range management. To say I was maxed out on all levels is an understatement.

Even though I appeared to be doing well on the outside, it wasn't long before I ran headlong into the brick wall of unresolved stuff from my childhood. At the end of my first year of college, I blew out my knee, and my basketball career ended. My relationship with my serious boyfriend also ended. I fell into the only coping strategy I knew—drinking. Also, around this time, my family lost our ranch and cow herd. This is a time in my life that I have blacked out and still do not have clear memories about what happened. I know that my dad asked me for money, and I gave him what cash I had set aside from gifts and prize money I had won in 4-H, rodeoing, and match racing my horses. All of us children together gave our dad more than sixty thousand dollars to help him cover the ranch's debt. We still lost everything.

As I started my second year in college, I could no longer play basketball because of the damage to my knee. I could no longer rodeo because I did not have enough money to pay for horse boarding, practice fees, travel, and entry fees. I was still a pre-vet, pre-med student, but without the tight schedule of eighteen to twenty credits per quarter plus two varsity sports, along with the loss of our ranch, my boyfriend, and one of my grandparents, I fell apart.

During that time, I lived in a house with my twin brother and four of his friends. Harlan, and his friends were accomplished drinkers, and I joined them. Soon, I fell further into the pit of my childhood trauma wounds. We had a barn and a place to keep horses at the place we were renting. One afternoon I was out riding, and I felt something snap in my groin area. It hurt so bad that I became nauseous. By sheer grit, I made it back to the barn and asked my brother to help me unsaddle and take me to the student health center. The doctor treated me with a large dose of antibiotics and gave me something for the pain. It was right before Thanksgiving, and I did not feel well enough to travel home to spend the holiday with my family. So, I stayed at our rental and took care of everyone's horses. While I was home alone and in severe pain, my emotional outlook fell further into the pit of despair. I could not move or ride or escape my agony, and I was not used to being stuck in such physical pain on top of my usual emotional pain. This was the first time I contemplated suicide. My perspective on life was that everything was dark and dire. I was living in a house where the previous occupant had committed suicide. I could no longer compete in the sports that I loved. My mom's life was totally off the rails, and she was drinking more than ever. My dad was in the dumps because he had lost the ranch. I talked to God and told him that I had been kind and loving to everyone around me and that I still felt horrible inside. Something was wrong. I told him I wanted to come home and that I was thinking about making that transition happen.

This was the first time my desire to not live became so present in my consciousness that I had to face my inner pain and desires. I felt like God had sent me to the wrong place. In this life, I had not become acquainted with God through an outer religion. I always knew God and had started talking to him when I felt alone as a small child, which was most of the time. I felt secure talking to God when I was outside riding or just being with my horses. I talked to God in somewhat the same voice I developed from my relationship with my dad. I mostly felt loved, accepted, and seen by my dad, and I pressed the envelope with him and usually told him what I was thinking or feeling even if I knew he would not necessarily approve. So, I approached God the Father in the same tone and told him I did not like being on Earth and I wanted to come home to him.

I got really sick. I didn't have much money and did not want to go back to the doctor. I stayed home by myself over the holiday weekend, and at one point, I realized I was sick enough to die. I told God I was ready and again that I wanted to come home. I believe God could have taken me home at that time. Then it dawned on me that I had not accomplished my purpose for living. I was only twenty-one. I then humbly asked God if I could stay and promised that I would start leading a spiritual life in which I loved him all the time. I sometimes see this experience metaphorically as a baby lightning strike that shocked me into moving toward the right path. It was a gradual process, but I stopped drinking so much and started talking to God daily.

Several months after my come-to-Jesus moment, I was inwardly led to seek further medical treatment for the horrible pain I was still experiencing. After consulting with several doctors, the gynecologist decided to do exploratory laparoscopic surgery. He discovered scar tissue from a ruptured ovarian cyst and told me I was fortunate I did not develop a serious infection from the rupture that had occurred while I was riding months before. My mom drove over to Bozeman to take care of me after the surgery even though I told her I did not want her to come.

Around this time, I also connected with a group for children of alcoholics. This was my first experience seeking help, understanding, and emotional support from a professional in a group setting. I read Claudia Black's books about children of alcoholics and shared for the first time about my nightmare experiences with my mom and my deep concerns about her drinking herself to death.

I was in my early twenties, struggling with unfinished business surrounding my childhood trauma from both my mom's and the neighbor boy's abuse. I had already followed in my mom's footsteps and was using alcohol as a means of escape from my inner pain. I was financially broke. Both my outer and inner life were hard, and the path forward seemed impossible.

I struggled, but I remembered my vow to God. Without being able to escape via sports and taking hard college courses, I gradually shifted toward living a life with a tiny bit of spiritual connection. I still had my horses, and when I spent time with them, I naturally felt connected to Spirit. As a child, I had attended summer Bible camp with Catholic nuns in Zortman. I regularly played in their beautiful church that was on a high hill. It was there that I fell in love with Mother Mary and often daydreamed about being a nun with my life devoted to her service. My parents were raised Lutheran, and I understood from them that we were not supposed to adore Mother Mary; it was akin to idolatry. But I did it anyway because I could not help loving her—I so wanted to be loved by a mother. Despite my early longings to be a nun when I played in the church, I moved away from that desire in my high school years, instead using striving and success as a means to avoid my inner spiritual longing and pain.

Now, in college, both my outer striving in playing basketball and rodeoing were off the table due to my knee injury and lack of finances. I was stuck just attending college, which was not enough scaffolding to keep me distracted from my inner turmoil. At times, I slid back into drinking, which of course was the prevalent social activity during college. Even though I was teetering back and forth between developing an inner spiritual practice and self-medicating with alcohol, I mostly persevered by trying to keep my promise to God—to find and live my reason for being.

My first summer after starting college, I attended horseshoeing school in Bozeman. It was a twelve-week course in which I learned how to trim a horse's hooves, shape horseshoes to fit them, and blacksmith horseshoes in a forge from a straight piece of iron. At this time, I still had hopes of becoming a horse veterinarian and wanted to specialize in lameness issues. Also, I loved the physicality of working with horses all day. During this time, I learned that I had a special talent for being able to see a horse's hoof once, correctly determine the length of steel necessary to make a shoe, then shape that shoe to be ready to nail onto the hoof. There is a contest for this called the eagle eye forging contest. I won it several times against horseshoer blacksmiths who had been shoeing for many years—compared to my mere months of experience.

The summer after my second year of college, I applied and was chosen for an apprenticeship at the horseshoeing shop at the New Bolton Center in Chester County, Pennsylvania. The Center is connected to the University of Pennsylvania Veterinary School and has been at the forefront of equine medicine for many years. I drove myself across the country in my green 1977 manual transmission truck—with only the company of my cow dog Teddy Bear. I found a place near the center to rent a room in an old house and got a job mucking stalls at a neighboring barn that housed horses competing in jumping events. My days were filled with shoveling manure and shoeing horses at the center.

While I was there, I had the opportunity to go out on a round of calls with a local veterinarian, who was a woman. The area was home to many fancy horses that competed in hunter or other jumping contests along the East Coast. The veterinarian seemed very grouchy and unhappy as we made our rounds to several fancy barns. After that experience, I was not so sure I wanted to be a veterinarian. Also, my dad had been advising me against going to vet school because he said it was very difficult physical work. He also did not like me shoeing horses and told me that I should be using my brains, not my brawn. I told him, "Surely, I will starve to death if I follow your advice."

On the way home from Pennsylvania that summer in our pickup truck, Teddy Bear and I suffered without air conditioning—the temperature was in the high nineties as we drove across the country. Sometimes I stopped to get him a scoop of ice cream to cool off since the inside of the pickup was so miserably hot even with the windows down. During one of these stops, I had my first experience of praying for someone I did not know. As I was walking back to the car after getting Teddy Bear's treat, I noticed a woman who seemed very stooped over, almost as if with sadness. I decided to experiment with praying for her and asking God to relieve her burden. After praying for her, I noticed that her step quickened and that she seemed almost lighter in her appearance.

I soon realized that I needed to alternate each quarter between attending college and working to make the money I needed. During the summers, I had my own business as a horseshoer and blacksmith. I loved the art of blacksmithing and helping horses move in balance by shoeing them correctly. During the day, I would shoe or trim between four to seven horses, which is very hard work. Then I would run home, take a shower, try to remove the dirt from under my fingernails, put on a skirt, and transform into a barmaid/bartender at a somewhat upscale bar in my hometown of Lewistown. My shift would start at five in the evening, and I would work until after one in the morning. The next morning, I would be out to someone's ranch by eight to shoe horses.

Sometimes, after shoeing seven horses in one day, I found that my hands hurt so badly I could hardly hold my fork to eat dinner. When I started my bar shift, my legs were already worn out, and I would wonder how I could possibly stand on my feet for another eight hours.

I wanted to finish my college education and was determined not to give up, so I just kept putting one foot in front of the other to finish whatever job was in front of me.

During some of the quarters I took off from attending college to make money, the bartending gig was not available. So, at times I waitressed, and for several months I worked as the night janitor at the same facility where I had bartended. In some ways, I liked being a janitor because I did not have to deal with people, but it was also very hard physical work.

Another summer I worked for my friend Wes, who had a business artificially inseminating (AI) cows. My job was to ride my horse among the cow herd and find the cows that indicated by their behavior they were hormonally ready to be bred. The first time I helped AI cows, I was five years old, helping my dad on our family ranch. So, by this time I had at least fifteen years of experience observing bovine behavior to determine which ones were ready to be bred. Once I found the cows that were ready, my horse and I had the job of rounding them up and putting them in a steel-paneled corral that was erected in the pasture.

My number-one horse that summer was my team roping heading horse Hank. *Heading horse* means that I rode him and roped the head of steers and then my partner roper would rope the steer's heels. Hank was a powerfully made red bay Quarter Horse. He was one of the last horses my mom and dad had bought for me. I also match-raced him, and, like Lisa, he had never been defeated in a race. I had won hundreds of dollars with the two of them.

One day, Wes asked me to get a cow into the corral. In arrogance, I told him "No problem." I thought to myself, *I have been doing this forever, I will show him.* I headed out to sort out this cow, and it started trotting and then running. Unlike in the movies, a good ranch hand never chases cows if it can be helped. We try to move them by lining ourselves up with them many feet away to keep them from running.

Sometimes, the cows do not cooperate, and the cow Wes wanted me to corral was one of those cows. She kept on running faster and faster. I tried to hold Hank back so that we could position ourselves to influence the cow to go in the right direction, but Hank had other plans. Pretty soon, Hank and I were following the cow at a breakneck pace across the field, making very hard, tight turns. I was terrified that I might not be able to stay on top of Hank. He was oblivious to my pulling on the reins. Finally, Hank succeeded in the task of corralling the cow with me still on top of him, hanging on to the saddle horn for dear life. Wes looked at me and said, "I never want to see you run a cow like that again." I felt humiliated, angry, and terrified, and all I could say was, "Please shut up, or you will have a crying cowgirl on your hands."

∞

CHAPTER 4

Spiritual Mother

∞

It was during one of my quarters matriculating at MSU that I first discovered outer spiritual teachings that matched my inner knowing. These teachings talked about the Lost Teachings of Jesus and how he taught that each of us has a divine connection and that we were each created in God's image. I understood that each of us has our own unique, divine geometry and no two of us are alike, similar to snowflakes.

In the book *The Path of the Higher Self*, authors Mark L. Prophet and Elizabeth Clare Prophet teach that climbing the internal, eternal summit of being is God's truth. I first read this book when I was twenty-four. They wrote, "We uphold, as God does, the right of every man to choose the path he shall take to the Summit of his own being. Although we cannot make the journey for him, we would offer a hand to help him on the way. The climber will need ropes and picks to scale the jagged heights. These we have provided, together with maps and charts to assist him in avoiding the pitfalls and unmarked ways where danger lurks and where those who have 'words without knowledge' may perish."[1]

I read these teachings published by Summit Lighthouse with an inner hunger and felt their truth throughout my being. My studies of these teachings initiated a daily practice of invoking light through prayer, but because I was a neophyte on the spiritual path, I made very slow progress toward embodying wholeness. One of the other first books by these authors that I read was *The Science of the Spoken Word*, and I learned that saying prayers out loud in a certain rhythm with heartfelt compassion could change my world. Since I was a pre-med student and studying science in my college courses at the time, I decided to do an experiment using the concepts in the book. I sat in an easy chair in the living room of my parents' house and proceeded to say each prayer thirty-three times. This practice took me longer than three hours. I focused on spiritual help for my mom, who was still a raging alcoholic. Soon after my experiment, something changed, and I witnessed positive results. My mom's life was better for a time. I decided to continue applying the science of the spoken prayerful word and began a daily practice that continues to this day.

I also became friends with several people who were studying the teachings too. They seemed a bit weird to me, not because of their religious studies, but because they were from California. I was in my early twenties and still very much a cowgirl from rural Montana. I had traveled to the East Coast by myself, but I still had a fairly narrow awareness of people from different cultural and geographical areas. My new friends had something inside them that drew me past my knee-jerk reaction to the differences that first seemed to separate us. I remember how much I loved watching one of the women cook. For some reason, the process of her lovingly preparing food for her family was deeply moving and peaceful to me.

I watched my new friends with an eagle eye to see if I could spot anything about them that would corroborate my first inclination not to trust them. My watchfulness provided me with evidence of their humanness. But more than anything, I saw and felt their contact with something beyond themselves. I saw their humble desire to be one with their divine path. I wanted what they had—a spiritual path forward.

I started my spiritual practice and path where I was. I was a financially broke college student with a budding addiction to alcohol. I was also addicted to being busy and focusing on outer success. These habits were well-developed and had already formed deep habitual grooves in my personality. My go-to defense was to be tough, to not need anyone else, and to try to do everything myself. I did not want to let anybody close because I did not want to get hurt.

After reading several Summit Lighthouse books, I realized that I had to forgive myself, and my mom too. But I was not yet ready to do that. I also learned that when I said prayers or decrees out loud, I could bring forth the vibration of the violet flame, which is for transmutation or transformation. I felt a warmth enter my being and even my physical cells felt uplifted and bathed in light. So I practiced my newfound spiritual awareness and applied the science of the spoken word to those things that I understood in my outer awareness to need changing. My life did change, and I noticed that those spirals of intense longing to leave Earth and go home to God happened less often and with less intensity.

I had no desire to find a spiritual teacher, especially not a woman. At that time, I feared allowing any woman to have any power over me. My view of the outer world was deeply skewed by my childhood trauma. I felt like I was doing fine by simply experimenting with applying the teachings to my life and casually seeing if my spiritual practice changed me or my life. And I was certainly not looking for a spiritual community. I preferred the company of my horses and dogs, and even though I wanted to love other people, in my outer mind, I did not want to depend on other people for anything.

One day one of my friends, who also studied the same teachings, asked if I wanted to borrow her new car to go to a church service led by Elizabeth Clare Prophet, the founder of the Church Universal and Triumphant. She could not go herself because she was sick, and I did want to drive my friend's fancy new car, but part of me was also scared to go because I had heard about cults and how they liked to take advantage of people. Now, I had no reason to believe that these people who were studying the same teachings as me were part of a cult, but it seemed that an inordinate number of them were from California. I searched within, and in my inner dialogue realized that, based on what I knew about myself, I was not likely to end up brainwashed. Also, so far, my experiments with applying the teachings had changed my inner and outer life. I decided it was safest to explore when I was by myself because I trusted my gut and my heart to determine whether I was in the right place. Plus, I had some experience as I had already been to several different church services as I searched for a spiritual path that was a fit.

When I arrived, I first entered a house near the building where the service would be held. In the living room, there was an elderly woman who looked and sang like an angel. Those of us gathered were invited to sing a song to our Holy Christ Self—the part of us that is one with Jesus Christ. The song raised me up, and I felt tingles and warmth throughout my being. I felt filled with love.

After the song, I was sitting in the living room and noticed a woman with her back to me. It seemed to me she had the world on her shoulders. It was my habit when I saw someone that looked burdened to say a prayer for them in my heart, so I prayed for this woman. All of a sudden, she turned and looked right at me. As I met her gaze, I realized that I had been sending a drop of God's love to the ocean of God's love. Even though she was small in physical stature, I could see the huge amount of light and love she carried in her presence. We both stared at each other for what could have been minutes, but in some ways felt like an eternity. We did not speak. There was no need to talk because I learned as much in that exchange between our eyes as I have in any conversation in my life.

The people who lived in the church's community called this woman Mother. To me, it was like calling a priest or pastor Father—since she was the leader of this church, they called her Mother. After that day, I learned that the title Mother was also a mantle or a spiritual office that she held in her service to all life. My first reaction to calling her Mother was that it seemed weird to me. But I felt a deep love and connection to her, so I was willing to experiment and test her and the community.

The church service I attended after meeting Mother was in an old milking barn that had been remodeled into a sanctuary. I loved the service, and as I went to my car afterward, I laughed inside as I realized that my fears about brainwashing were based on my small self. Nobody had tried to stop me, nobody had tried to convert me, and I was free to come and go as I wanted. All I had experienced was the uplifting love of God through singing and prayers that allowed that love to flow into the physical realm.

My inner direction changed for a time. I was no longer so driven to pursue my college education—I wanted to take time to follow my heart and look into these teachings. I heard about a twelve-week course called Summit University that was held at the church's campus near Los Angeles. The description of the course said students would learn about the mystical traditions of many of the world's religions. My heart was pulling me to attend Summit, but I was worried about paying for myself. My parents were very broke at this time, and while I wanted to be able to help them if I could, I also wanted to get away, spread my wings, and follow my heart.

To make enough money to travel and attend the course, I worked multiple jobs, including returning to bartending. Even though I worked around the clock, I barely made enough money to cover my expenses and the fees to attend Summit University. A friend who bartended with me offered me the opportunity to ride to Arizona with her and her mother, which saved me the expense of an airplane ticket.

I left on Christmas Eve and arrived at my destination in California on December 28, 1985, to attend the New Year's conference, Teachings from the Mystery School. The spiritual teachings at the conference transported me into the heavens, and I felt the love of God throughout my being. We sang many songs, including "God Is Real in Me," a title that reflected how my internal horizons were altered during my twelve-week retreat.

The church's campus and the place where I stayed at night were both in much more populated areas than I had ever spent time in before. I missed my horses and the great outdoors of Montana. Yet, I met other students from around the world and made friends that I love to this day. Also, the campus was located a hike's distance from some horses.

I stayed until after Easter 1986 and then returned home to my parents' house. Returning was particularly hard because I was no longer used to my mom's dramatic swings with her alcoholism. I struggled with seeing my dad working so hard to find a way to pay his remaining debt. I felt like I could not solve either my mom's or my dad's problems. So, I prayed for them and loved them.

Several months after returning home, I felt called to serve at the church's Inner Retreat. The church had purchased property near Yellowstone Park and was in the process of constructing a new ranch campus there. I filled out and sent in my application. I was offered a position leading a team working with the church's cows. One of my first discussions with my boss was about what my work title should be. I realized that I was new to the community and younger than all the others on my team. But I knew that my experience growing up on ranches in Montana and studying range management and pre-veterinary medicine at MSU qualified me to lead the team. Still, I did not want to come in and be elevated above those who had been there before my arrival. So my boss and I agreed that I could have the title "cow boss." I think he thought I would be embarrassed by it, but it was fine with me.

My time as the cow boss at the church ended up being three of the best years of my life. Several other women assisted me with almost all the work with the cows. One summer, my friend Deborah and I spent long days in the forest moving—or mostly searching for—cows. We were often at elevations well above a mile, and our days were filled with glorious scenery. Each day was a new adventure together as we moved through the landscape, observing the wildlife. Since I had the most experience, I rode with a 30-30 rifle under my right leg. I always wondered what I was supposed to do if I saw a bear—it seemed impossible that I would be able to shoot from my horse to save my friend. Thank goodness I never had to use my rifle!

Each day, we started with 5:00 a.m. prayers, decrees, and meditations. Then Deborah and I would grab food and saddle up while the morning was still cool. We often did not get out of the mountains until after dinner. Most evenings, we either had prayer service or spiritual studies. It seemed like heaven to be on horseback high in the mountains, moving cows each day, with ample opportunity to pray and study spiritual teachings.

My horse at the time was Prince, a five-year-old red roan draft cross. We had been on a trip to purchase ranch horses, and Prince had been standing off to the side, barely green-broke. I liked him from the first moment I saw him. I decided that there had to be a prince inside him somewhere and bought him for hardly anything. Even though Prince was not very well trained, he loved me and I loved him. I often felt like I had been with Prince for lifetimes and pretended that he was my pet elephant in India from a past life.

One day, Deborah and I saddled up early, and she asked to ride Prince. Since he was doing very well as my riding horse, I told Deborah she could. Several hours into our day, I looked across the high mountain meadow and saw Prince running off and heard Deborah hollering at me. They were too far away for me to really do anything, but I needed to do something to try to keep both Prince and Deborah from getting hurt. I called out "Whoa, Prince." He heard me and changed his direction, running right to me and stopping close by. He was scared and wanted me to help him. Once Prince was near me, he and Deborah were both safe.

Deborah and I had so much fun working together in the high country. As there was so much land to cover, sometimes we would spend all day looking for a single cow. One day, when we found the cows, we noticed that one of them was limping. We decided we needed to doctor it. I had years of experience roping in an arena, but I had not roped much out on the open range, and Deborah did not know how to rope at all. It was up to me to catch the cow and secure her so we could doctor her safely. I somehow roped her head and tied that rope to one tree and then roped her hind feet and stretched her between two trees. While the cow was safely tied between the trees, Deborah was able to give her an injection of antibiotics. Next, I had to figure out how to get both of my ropes off this big cow without getting hurt. Through ingenuity, great teamwork, and the much-needed grace of God, Deborah and I accomplished that cow-doctoring task and many others.

Another much sadder story about Deborah and me involves my cow dog Teddy Bear. One morning, we had started riding at daybreak, and by the time the sun was rising, we were already on top of a high butte. I remember riding along, watching the sunrise, and thanking God for the gift of the day, my friend Deborah, my horse, and my good dog. I felt so blessed.

Later in the day, we had completed our work on the butte and made it to the lower meadow, which was crisscrossed with irrigation ditches full of water. As I was riding along, Teddy Bear jumped into a ditch to cool off, and when I focused on him, I saw he was in a whirlpool, getting sucked into a culvert. Our eyes connected for what seemed like forever—and for the last time. He was sucked into the culvert and got stuck in the debris inside. When he finally popped out the other side, even though I tried mouth-to-nose resuscitation, it was too late for Teddy Bear. I was very shocked by his loss and wondered why God would allow my sweet and faithful dog to die.

My all-women team worked very hard, day and night, sometimes taking care of the church's livestock. The church had purchased a herd of Black Angus cows that seemed to have had tough times before they came to us. Some of the cows were a little skinny, and all of them acted like they had not been treated kindly by their previous owner. During calving season, I often walked through the herd, checking to see which cows were getting close to giving birth. Some of the cows would "take me," which in cowgirl language means they tried to charge me and mow me down with their heads. I carried a two-foot-long stick, and when they charged, I would hit them between the ears until they quit.

But despite being only twenty-four and seemingly bulletproof, one day my bravado got punctured. A cow came after me, and no matter how much I pounded her on the head with the stick, she kept coming. Thank goodness I was still athletic because I was able to outrun her and hop over a nearby fence. She got close to hitting me in multiple places, but she missed. I was never as courageous after that while walking through the herd during calving season.

Even in what often seemed like heaven on Earth, I sometimes experienced people problems. My supervisor was a good man, but he had never run a ranch before, and he doubted my all-women team. We were taking care of more than five hundred mother cows and their calves in a feedlot on the ranch. This was a lot for two people to take care of, especially in the spring when the cows are calving and need extra care, so we asked for more help. He thought we were just whining. We were working fifteen-hour days, doing hard physical work, sometimes even working at night in the cold and snow. Since I was the leader of my team, I went above my supervisor's head to Mother, who was also the president of the church.

Her assistant set up a meeting for me and Mother. Even though I was driven to solve the work problem for my team, I became overwhelmed with my childhood trauma. My unresolved emotional pain surfaced so suddenly and tumultuously that I had to take a few days off because I could not function. I canceled my meeting with Mother because I could not be the leader that I wanted to be. I could not handle the leadership responsibilities to care for my team because I was not whole enough.

I felt so disappointed in myself. Mother had been kind to me, and I knew she was straightforward and would do her best to fulfill her responsibilities to run the church. Still, my consciousness was being hijacked by my fears and terror left over from my childhood. I reached deep inside and searched my soul. As part of my endeavor to understand what was going on inside me, I wrote a letter to my angels and asked for divine guidance. I then burned this letter as a ritual of releasing my desire for direction. The morning after I sent the letter by fire, I woke up feeling like part of me had been transplanted to the East Coast. I felt like, even though I knew my body was physically in Paradise Valley, Montana, parts of me had already left and were now residing somewhere else. My inner direction or intuition seemed to inform me that my next, best step was to follow those parts of my consciousness that already had moved on to my next place to be. I felt so strange and out of sorts that I wrote a letter to Mother explaining my inner crisis and feelings. She immediately responded, and her assistant telephoned me with her words. She said my resignation was accepted. I quickly wrote back and said I did not mean to resign and that I loved my job. Mother wrote back and said, "Your prompting was correct."

When I chose to follow the promptings of my heart, it seemed like all hell broke loose inside me. My unresolved feelings of fear and terror from childhood rose up, and dark feelings of doom rained down on my head. I felt like dark ravens were dive-bombing me with cascading feelings and thoughts of inadequacy, doubts, and fear of not having enough money to eat and take care of myself. These thoughts were so intense that I felt overwhelmed and frozen at times. I had been inspired by God to follow my heart and leave all that I knew behind me, and as a result, I was stuck in the greatest amount of darkness that I had ever felt. I feared I might lose my mind.

Within two weeks of writing to the angels and then to Mother, I was packed up and on my way across the United States to Philadelphia to study journalism and become a writer. During my time as cow boss at the church's ranch, I had written several letters to editors of local and statewide newspapers regarding natural resource issues impacting rural Montana. My letters were printed as op-eds, and several people told me I should become a writer. I followed my heart and decided to leave my cowgirl life and spiritual community behind to learn how to be a better communicator.

I chose the East Coast because, on some level, my heart preceded me there. Also, I thought the policymakers who had the power to influence natural resource policy in the West were ignorant of the on-the-ground impacts of their poor thinking and arrogant in their approach. I did not want to suffer from the same afflictions, so I decided I needed to live and learn among the East Coast decisionmakers. I wanted to understand where these people—who thought they knew more about the West than those who lived there—were coming from. I wanted to walk in their footprints and see if I could bridge the gap to resolve the outer issues that split people from the West and East.

I felt very insecure and unsure of myself. I reached out to my dad for support, and he gave me a little money and a ride part of the way East, across Montana to an airport in North Dakota. But he also told me that I couldn't just move to the East Coast to finish my education—I didn't have any money. I felt angry that he was trying to tell me I couldn't do what I wanted to do. So, once again, I stiffened my resolve and told him that I would wash hospital floors to make enough money to finish my schooling. I would become a writer.

I had so many things activated inside me at that time because, in addition to the anger at my dad, I also felt dark thoughts and fear rising up and cascading down on me. While I was traveling with my dad in his car, it was all I could do to hold it together. I felt like I was in the middle of a holographic ping-pong game of conflicting thoughts and feelings. Even though I wanted his support, I chose not to mention my inner turmoil, as it did not seem like he would be supportive. He did not like my involvement with the church, so I figured he would blame my internal state on them. So, I bucked up, moved forward, and hoped my internal weather would clear, or that I would at least see the sun again.

Upon arriving in Pennsylvania, I moved into the church's teaching center in Bryn Mawr, a suburb of Philadelphia. At first, I worked as a server in a little restaurant and then moved up to assistant manager.

While I was saving up some money, I applied to reenter college. My applications were accepted at the University of Pennsylvania and Temple University. I chose Temple because it was more affordable, and I was still financially broke after living and serving at the church's ranch for three years.

Most of my credits from MSU transferred, and so I embarked on one and half years of studying journalism, communication, and the arts, all of which I had not studied during my pre-med years. During my time at Temple, I wrote op-eds for the student newspaper. I recently uncovered an old one that read, "I used to be in solitude amongst thirty thousand acres, and now I am amongst thirty thousand people in less than an acre." My transition from being a cowgirl in Montana to living in urban Philadelphia was hard and scary, and I often shed tears of homesickness.

Fresh from the range, the only clothes I owned were from my ranch workdays, which did not seem appropriate for my job in downtown Philadelphia or attending classes at Temple. My aunt, with whom I had lived when I had been an intern at the New Bolton Veterinary Center's horseshoeing shop, took me shopping. She bought me a skirt, several tops, and a pair of pants suitable for my job at the Temple University Press. I did not have a suitable pair of shoes; my footwear was exclusively cowboy boots and tennis shoes. My mom sent me an old pair of her dress shoes, which did not fit very well. I walked or used public transportation to get around because I did not own a car. While walking, I promised myself that when I had money, I would never again wear ill-fitting shoes.

At this point in my life, my feet were not the only part of me feeling extreme discomfort. Leaving everything I loved, the sanctity of the church ranch, and Montana was very hard for me. As soon as I decided to leave, a mountain of self-doubt and even terror threatened to overwhelm me. If Mother had not moved so quickly to accept my resignation and nudge me out of my safety zone at the ranch, I would not have been able to continue. I had also sold much of my shoeing and ranching equipment to fund my trip. The truth was that I couldn't go back if I had wanted to; the door was closed.

My internal warring with extreme fear and doubt continued for years. Oftentimes, I felt very lost because my background growing up on ranches in Montana was so different than living in downtown Philadelphia on North Broad Street across from Temple University, a historically Black area of town. One time, I was in the grocery store where I was most likely the only white person. When I got to the cash register, I did not have enough money to pay for my groceries—I had made a mistake in my math. (I was so broke I often ate Special K cereal for several meals in a day, and I tried to be very careful with every penny I spent.) With a long line of women behind me, I felt mortified that I could not pay. I wanted to hide my face and run out of the store. A lovely Black woman behind me in line reached out and gave me the few dollars I was short so that I could pay. I was so grateful for her kindness.

During the two years of finishing my bachelor's degree at Temple, even though I borrowed money through school loans, I also worked several different jobs to pay for expenses. Sometimes, I delivered newspapers from four to seven in the morning and then went to my classes. After class, I worked at a free-market think-tank doing research. Also, since I was a journalism student, I was always looking for an opportunity to get my stories published and would seek out writing assignments. One time, I delivered a newspaper containing a story I had written—my life passion and my day job colliding in a full-circle moment.

I often felt like I was on a never-ending treadmill of work, before and after my classes, as well as serving at the church's teaching center, including cleaning duties and cooking for those who attended church service. I also engaged in four to fifteen hours of prayer each week in efforts to help protect America and solve world problems. I went from one task to another without a day off for months. I had been an honor roll student in much of my past studies, yet I was weakest in English and writing. I had been allowed to skip English classes in high school because I could read and comprehend material at a level that was years beyond my grade level and had tested well in vocabulary. Unfortunately, I did not know how to diagram a sentence, and when I studied Spanish in college, I realized I had a pretty big hole in my education. This hole of not really understanding the basics of English became evident at Temple. But even with everything on my plate, I worked hard enough to get good grades and even made the honor roll for a few semesters.

During my time finishing college in Philadelphia, I missed Montana, and my heart ached to go home to the church's ranch. Sometimes, I felt so alone on my path that I would listen to Julie Andrews sing the songs from *The Sound of Music* over and over on my portable cassette player. Her voice and those songs soothed me and helped me navigate my feelings of aloneness, terror of being in the city instead of rural Montana, and fear of failure.

During my time at the teaching center, Mother and other members of the community were out traveling the country, sharing the message of walking in Christ's footsteps, and they came to visit. Mother stayed long after the service so she could talk with everyone who wanted to talk to her. I waited until everyone else was done, and she finally turned to me and asked, "Did you want to talk with me?" I said, "Oh, yes, Mother."

I told her I wanted to come home as soon as possible. She gently told me that my current direction was correct and that I should stay the course and finish my studies. I almost burst into tears. She reached out to hug me, but I did not let her. At some level, I felt dirty, and I did not want her to get dirty by touching me. I now know this feeling was most likely related to my being sexually abused as a child, even though this memory was not in my conscious mind at that time.

Shame lived inside me and was part of me.

Mother's loving support and kind but firm way of kicking me out of the nest helped me find the internal means to persevere and push forward to complete my journalism degree. I will always be grateful to her for seeing me as whole and then gently nudging me toward living from that wholeness.

∞

CHAPTER 5

Success and Starving

∞

After completing my degree in journalism, I moved back to Montana and started my own business as a freelance journalist. I would get on the phone and call two or three of the regional agricultural newspapers and sell them the same story, which they allowed as long as I wrote the story a little differently for each paper. This ended up being very good practice because I learned how to use the same facts to create several different stories. As I recall, the papers paid me less than fifty dollars per story, so once again I was broke, broke, broke.

Even though I was putting in long hours and hustling, I was not able to make enough money to pay all my bills. My school loans had to be paid each month, and I had other expenses. I could only afford to rent a one-room apartment in Livingston. I was living hand-to-mouth and could barely afford gas to travel to the places I had to go to research stories about rural Montana.

Since I needed a better job, I moved to Minneapolis, Minnesota. During my year-long stay in Minneapolis, I worked as a receptionist at Intel, as well as doing telemarketing in the evenings. I also worked as an executive assistant at a small business. Sometimes, I spent ten to twelve hours on the phone as a receptionist and then sold products in the evening. It was very hard to sit that long indoors, but I developed good phone skills and even became an adept salesperson.

There were some things I did not like about sales. One evening while I was selling books or some other product, the man who answered my call liked me. He seemed lonely and was willing to purchase whatever I was selling. I decided that I did not want to take advantage of his kindness, trust, and willingness to purchase from me and told him he probably did not need what I was selling. It just so happened one of the supervisors was listening, and I was chastised for not closing the sale. Before that evening, my competitive nature had helped me win several prizes for the most sales in an evening of calls. After that night, I could no longer convince people to spend money on things they did not need.

During my time in Minneapolis, my freelance writing career

continued to expand as I wrote at night or between my jobs on the weekends. I had graduated to writing bigger articles for agriculture magazines, and I was starting to make decent money. During the research phase for one of my stories, I called someone who worked on natural resource issues for the American Farm Bureau Federation in Washington, DC. When I introduced myself, I hurriedly told him that I grew up on a ranch, participated in 4-H and FFA, and rodeoed. I wanted him to know that I was not a biased journalist with no understanding of those who made their livelihoods from agriculture and out to write pieces that would hurt them and their communities. As soon as I came up for a breath, he asked if I was looking for a job. He went on to explain that the assistant editor for the Farm Bureau news had just left for another job and that they were looking to replace him. I asked where the job would be located, and he said that it was in Washington, DC. Though my internal dialogue said *hell no* at the thought of being back on the East Coast, another part said, *you need to look into this.*

During my time in Minneapolis, I shared a one-room apartment with two other women. I slept in the living room on a futon on the floor. We had no furniture besides our beds. Since I was working two and sometimes three jobs, I was starting to dig myself out of my lack of money. But I still did not have clothes suitable to interview for an office job in DC, so I called a friend who lent me money so I could purchase two suits to wear during my interviews.

Within a week of my first phone call with them, the Farm Bureau had flown me to DC so I could interview for the job. Within days of the interview, I received a good job offer. When the Farm Bureau offered to put me up in a hotel and give me sixty dollars a day for food, I thought I had died and gone to heaven. Also, they offered to pay for a truck to move all my belongings. I declined the offer, smiling inside and knowing that I probably should not share that all my belongings fit into my small Ford Escort that my great-uncle had recently given me money to purchase.

Part of me did not want to move to DC. The first Gulf War was in full swing, and I did not feel safe moving to the East Coast. I did not know anyone in DC. I was also afraid that I was not professional enough to work as an assistant editor on a national newspaper for Farm Bureau members. I had never done anything similar to this job. Even though I had these outer doubts, my inner prompting was to take on the challenge.

Just as when I moved to Philadelphia and my aunt had to buy me a few outfits so I could dress without looking like the Montana cowgirl that I was, I again did not have suitable clothing to wear to attend Congressional hearings and Supreme Court cases concerning agricultural issues. I only had the two suits I had bought for the interview process. Someone had shared the wisdom that I was better off purchasing a few items of quality clothing that would last rather than purchasing more items of lesser quality, so I did. As soon as I had a few extra dollars after starting the job, I went to Frugal Fannie's, a higher-end discount clothing store, and purchased several more business suits. For several years, I covered Congress as a journalist with only five or six different outfits.

Working in a big office in DC was a steep learning curve. Not only did I have to learn my profession, but I also had to learn office culture, which was very different than working with horses or chasing cows. I also needed to learn how to find my way around and survive in this new and very big city. When I first arrived in DC, an executive in my church had reached out to me and asked if I would lead the church's teaching center in DC. I declined because I was overwhelmed with my day job and the total change of environment. But after six grueling months and learning how to ride public transportation to get to and from work, where to buy groceries, and all the little things one has to learn when adjusting to a new life, I called her back and said I would take on the responsibility of leading the church group.

At this time, I was just twenty-eight years old, and the only leadership experience I had was when I was cow boss at the church's ranch, as well as in 4-H and FFA. The church once had a very strong community in the DC area, but this had changed and needed to be restored. The group didn't have its own space to meet and was renting space from a Buddhist group for Sunday services. The first thing I did was find a building that had adequate parking and was zoned to permit us to hold services there. My income was high enough for me to put down the deposit and insure payment of the rent.

The church allowed students of the teachings to join the community and live in the teaching center so long as they agreed to a spiritual lifestyle and to serve the center with prayers and household chores. At any given time, I had between three and six students, both men and women, living with me at the center. My service as the church's leader was also like that of a house mother—it was a great joy as well as hair-raisingly stressful. Each night, I went to bed with my heart empty because I had given away all the love and support that I possessed. Then, each morning, upon rising and doing my morning practice of prayers and decrees, I was filled again. I loved this time of my life. Again, I harkened back to Julie Andrew's character in *The Sound of Music* and pretended I was like her, taking care of motherless adult children. My experience of being filled up because I emptied myself in loving service to others forever reshaped my life.

Even though my life was filled with love and service, I struggled sometimes to keep awake at my job as a researcher, writer, and editor for one of the nation's premier agricultural policy newspapers. The demands of my church service left me physically tired, and I would need a nap so that I could be alert enough to write. Even though I did not want to get caught napping, sometimes I just had to lie down on my office floor and rest. I would shut the door and put my feet against it in hopes that if someone needed me, I could jump to my feet and look alert before they entered my office.

During the three years I worked for the American Farm Bureau Federation, I often covered hearings in the House or Senate, which meant that I would attend and take notes and photographs for our newspaper. I sometimes covered the cases that were being heard at the United States Supreme Court. In March of 1992, the Court heard arguments in Lucas v. South Carolina, which was a fifth amendment case. Property rights issues are extremely important to farmers and ranchers, so my boss sent me to the Supreme Court to cover the oral arguments—an experience that changed my life.

Prior to my preparation for reporting on this case, I had not paid much attention to court cases of any kind. While preparing to write this story though, I researched takings law and was flooded with memories of how horrible it was for my family to lose our ranch. Though we did not lose it in a government takings case, it was still a traumatic loss due to debt amid sky-high interest rates and inflation in the 1980s. Those factors, coupled with the tanking of the agricultural production economy, made this a very difficult period for American farmers.

Losing our family ranch was one of the times during the different traumas in my life that I lost time. I literally cannot remember days or weeks around the time the bank came and loaded up our cows to cover my dad's debt. While I revisited this period during my study of takings law, I realized I was passionate about property rights.

I was happy, extremely challenged, and professionally fulfilled with my job in DC. On the outer, there was no indication that I was about to make another life-changing decision. As I listened to the attorneys arguing the case, I realized that I wanted to argue cases, not just write about what happened while others argued. I was following the inner compass driving me forward, yet I knew I had to complete the necessary outer professional steps to be successful.

Soon after this assignment, I started studying to take the Law School Admissions Test (LSAT). I was nervous about taking it because I was in my late twenties and had never planned on going to law school. But I figured I could shoe a horse and had become a journalist covering Congress—I should be able to pass a test to get into law school. Even though I was following my heart, as when I had decided to leave the church ranch and move East, I once again felt the familiar cascades of terror. Looking back, I realize that there were many times in my life I moved forward to fulfill my inner direction even though I felt overwhelming fear and feelings of inadequacy.

The night before I took the LSAT for the first time, all hell broke out among the residents who lived at the teaching center with me. I felt like a mother whose four children all fell apart at the same time in personal crisis. When I arrived the next day to take the test, I was short of sleep and overstimulated because of the chaos at the center. When my score came back, it was not good enough for me to get into the law schools that I had my eyes on.

I scheduled to retake the exam and decided not to tell those who lived at the center. I figured that if they did not know I was taking a test so that I could leave DC and pursue my next step, maybe they wouldn't have personal crises that bled over into my life. It worked. I was able to sneak away, take the LSAT, and attain a good enough score to secure a place at various law schools. I began listening for inner direction on where I should apply. I decided to go back to my roots and applied to law school at the University of Montana and was accepted as an out-of-state student (since my current residence was in DC). My life was a whirlwind after attending that Supreme Court hearing in March because, by the fall of 1992, I had moved across the country and was living in Missoula, Montana, attending my first year of law school.

Moving home to Montana also meant I was closer to my aging parents, and it was a welcome change on my inner and outer path toward wholeness. In some ways, being in Montana seemed familiar. In other ways, it was a total launch into the unknown. I followed my passion to become an attorney to defend people and their property rights and livelihoods. It seems silly, but I had no awareness of the legal profession. During my first days of law school, I wondered what I had done to myself.

Before law school, I had always occupied the upper tier of outer intelligence as proven by my grades and performance in school, but I cannot say that I had worked that hard on my education. In fact, I was a bit intellectually lazy because I did not have to work that hard to be in the upper tier. Within a few hours of being on campus at law school though, I realized that my intellect was pretty pedestrian compared to the other students. Yet this realization was not daunting. When it came to sports, I had never been the most gifted, and somehow, I had found that through ingenuity and hard work, I could find a way to excel. I would do the same here.

I was thirty years old when I started law school. Most of the other students were in their mid-twenties. This age difference and my observations of the other students also helped me to realize that my ability to work hard would be a differentiating factor between me and my peers. Since I was older and already facing some health challenges, I understood that not only would I have to really apply myself, but I also had to figure out a way to work smarter.

The other thing I learned is that even though I had been a fierce competitor in sports, I was a powder puff compared to my law classmates. To me, they seemed pretty harsh in their competitive willingness to engage in oral argument in class. I felt lost and like I was getting run over repeatedly. I think this was due to my emphasis on spiritual studies and daily spiritual practice. Even though I did not want to surrender my goals of inner peace, harmony, and compassion, I knew that to succeed as an attorney, I would have to toughen up. Sometimes I felt like a deer in the headlights among a pack of wolves.

One time a group of my women classmates and I were talking, and for some reason, one of them asked me about my religious affiliation. I attempted to dodge the question and she persisted. So, I told the group that I was a member of Church Universal and Triumphant, and my classmates recoiled. The church had been the target of much negative media attention (it had been labeled a cult) and had even received shooting threats. Based on my past experiences with discrimination for being white on the reservation, looking "Indian" off the reservation, being white in a Black neighborhood in Philadelphia, and being a member of a church that had been targeted by the media, I was understandably reluctant to share my religious affiliation. The woman who had questioned me had held herself out as a fair, liberal (in the true sense of the word), and compassionate person. Immediately after the experience, I felt unsettled and shaken because I thought, *Here I go again. Another place where I will not fit in.* Later that evening, she called me and apologized, and we began a kind, open, respectful friendship that endures to this day. She also just happened to be the number one student in our class.

At the time I went to law school, there was no attendance policy. Since I had been admitted as an out-of-state student, I had to pay higher tuition until I could re-establish my residency. I also had to make money to pay for living expenses while I attended law school. Based on my experience of working at the American Farm Bureau Federation, the Montana Farm Bureau Federation hired me to write their newsletter and lobby at the state legislature. The Montana legislature meets every other year, and my first year of law school was one of the years it was in session.

I spent many evenings traveling back and forth to Helena, an hour-and-a-half drive from Missoula, during my first year of law school. The intellectual growth created by studying the law, coupled with the hard work at a job involving writing and sharing ideas, exponentially increased my ability to focus mentally. It took every erg of energy I could muster to process and understand my legal courses. But after finishing, or at least accomplishing the minimum amount of studying I needed, I then had to work on my job for the Farm Bureau.

Everything I wrote for them was for publication either by print or by way of my testifying at a hearing during the legislative session. It seemed I had no respite from striving to stretch my mind while having to craft language on what I was learning at the same time.

During the final exams at the end of my first semester, I woke up very sick one morning and was having difficulty breathing. I went to student healthcare, and a doctor diagnosed me with pneumonia, telling me I had to rest. I asked, "What about my finals?" The doctor told me that my first concern was breathing and allowing my body to heal. He wrote me a note for my professors so I could miss my finals. This was at least the sixth time I had been diagnosed with pneumonia, and realizing I could die, I surrendered and quit trying so hard. I prayed and asked for assistance because I was afraid of failing and dying.

What I realized through that prayer was that I had to seek balance and that I could not be the best at everything. I could only be the best at being me and excelling at living my life to its fullest. I was reminded of my winning the all-around cowgirl award several times in my teenage years. Winning the all-around meant I had excelled in multiple events at a rodeo, though I may not actually have won a single event. So, as I healed, I decided to be the best I could be within the constraints of a life that included working almost full-time while attending law school.

The professors told us that in the first year of law school, they scare us to death; in the second year, they work us to death; but by the third year, we ignore them. Even though I was stretched so thin, I still made personal achievements: I wrote a legal essay and was chosen to be on *Law Review* during my second year, which is a student-run publication and a prestigious accomplishment. Though that year, I did not have to travel to Helena several times a week because it was an off year for the legislature, I still had way too much work to do. Being on the *Law Review* was almost as much work as a full-time job. And

I was still writing the Montana Farm Bureau newsletter and publishing op-ed articles in various state newspapers to educate people about policy issues impacting agriculture.

During my third year of law school, I again traveled back and forth to Helena. That year, I lobbied for and helped pass property rights legislation that another law student and I had drafted and shared with the bill's sponsor during my first year of school. Also, I was co-editor-in-chief of the *Montana Law Review*, which meant I was responsible for leading our student team to choose essays and edit them for publication. That year the dean of the law school arranged for his friends, who were the top scholars on religious freedom, to come for a symposium on the First Amendment. We edited and published these essays in the *Law Review* that year. And the United States Supreme Court cited an edition of our team's *Montana Law Review* during one case in which they ruled on religious freedom.

By this time, I was almost thirty-three and exhausted from working the equivalent of what seemed like three full-time jobs: attending law school, editing the *Montana Law Review*, and working for the Farm Bureau. Also, I was getting tired of attending class with those whose intellectually aggressive tendencies had been put on steroids during law school. I had not abandoned my spiritual life and practices, but I made adjustments. I decided to eat more red meat and adopted some of my past outer toughness from my history as an athletic competitor because I found being with my classmates sometimes painful at multiple levels.

As I pushed so hard on the outside to master what I needed to learn to enter the legal profession, I struggled inside. I did not like who I had become to succeed in the law school culture. I also ignored my unresolved pain because I could not afford to feel, process, or let anyone see my vulnerability.

During graduation, I walked down the aisle with Justice Sandra Day O'Connor, who gave the commencement address in 1995. She loved to fly fish and was in Montana from Washington, DC for a fishing vacation. I do not remember much from that day, but I clearly remember her sharing with us that for her, law was like music, and every note mattered. Her words, mixing art with her impressions from being a Supreme Court Justice, have often buoyed me up in my professional journey practicing law.

The extreme inner and outer climb necessary to become a lawyer does not end at graduation. The next step was studying for the bar exam so I could be licensed to practice law. A private business offered a course that most graduates took over the summer to prepare for the bar exam in August, but I was so burned out from my harsh experience that I could not make myself attend any more classes. I felt like I had PTSD (post-traumatic stress disorder) or had been brainwashed—yet I knew I had to pass the bar exam.

Around this time, I attended a seminar on mind mapping and how certain people absorbed information better using this method. I decided to take a risk and do my own kinder, more artsy method of study in preparation for the bar exam. I bought myself some colored markers and some large, blank pieces of paper. I listened to my favorite baroque music while diagraming my study material in mind maps. I felt like a child again in art class. My inner enthusiasm returned, and I felt prepared for the exam.

On the third day of the exam, I experienced grueling pelvic pain. It hurt so badly that I almost couldn't finish. I forced myself to push the pain out of my mind and used all my might to focus so that I would not fail and have to wait for another year and spend more money to take the exam again. I simply could not afford, on any level, to flunk the test. My ability to push my body and mind entered a whole new realm that day. I denied my own needs and pains to push forward to become a professional in the legal field. I found out several months later that I passed the exam. But the pain stayed with me as a constant reminder of the stress and pressure I was under. It was reminiscent of the ovarian cyst that had ruptured when I was a teen, but it was much worse and dispersed throughout my pelvic area. Later, the pain would be diagnosed as severe endometriosis.

Back in my second year of law school, my classmates and I began searching for our first legal jobs to start after graduation and passing the bar exam. Competition for that first legal job is extreme. During my time working as a journalist in Washington, DC, I had heard then–Chief Judge Loren A. Smith give a talk to the Federalist Society and had been mesmerized by his intellect, kind heart, and passion regarding property rights and the law.

When it came to the job search, I simply followed my heart, sending him, along with letters of recommendation, a simple letter stating it was my dream job to clerk for him. Smith's clerk scheduled the Chief Judge and me for a phone interview, as the United States Court of Federal Claims did not pay travel expenses for interviews and I did not have enough money to pay for a trip to DC and back. During the interview, somehow our discussion went far afield from a typical interview for a clerkship. After I hung up, I thought, *Either that went really well or I bombed it.* Instead of being buttoned-up and lawyer-like, he asked me about my childhood growing up on ranches in Montana. I recounted numerous wild stories about what my siblings and I did and how we barely escaped death or injury many times.

Soon, the Chief Judge sent me an offer—I was his first hire that year. Since he was the chief judge, he could hire up to three clerks. I learned later how prestigious it was for me to be his number-one hire when I clerked at the Court. Early on in my clerkship, all the judges for the Court of Federal Claims and their law clerks gathered for a luncheon. Since my judge was the most senior, he would introduce his law clerks last. I started to feel totally out of place as the judges introduced their clerks as having gone to upper-tier or Ivy League colleges for undergrad, and some were graduates of Harvard or Yale Law School. I started to squirm as I waited for Chief Judge

Smith's turn to introduce his law clerks, and worried about what he would say about me.

When Judge Smith got to me, the last clerk to be introduced since I was his first hire, he said, "This is Hertha Lund, the state champion horseshoer from Montana." I do not remember what else he said, but I was a bit mortified and felt like I did not measure up. However, during my time with Chief Judge Smith, I realized that he was very proud of my background—he was happy to employ someone who was not cut from the same seemingly prestigious cloth as many of the others. My judge enjoyed promoting me as a ranch girl from Montana who had worked hard to earn a job at the court.

I loved being in chambers with and learning from Chief Judge Smith. As his clerk, it was my job to read all the briefs, discuss issues with him, and assist him in drafting his orders or opinions, which he would then revise to his liking. Working on legal briefs with the Chief Judge was like driving a Ferrari for the day. I knew he had forgotten more about property rights and takings law than I might ever know.

Even though I loved working with the Chief Judge and felt accepted and appreciated by him, I felt out of place among the other law clerks. One of them was a woman from New Jersey, who was lovely in every way. She was very polished, smart, and beautiful; had gone to the best schools; and seemed to be everything I was not. I saw myself through her eyes, a frumpy Montana cowgirl, and I realized I could try and compete with her and lose, or I could ask her for help.

She first helped by making hair and makeup appointments for both of us at a chic beauty salon in Georgetown. When we arrived, I was handed off to the stylish European owner. He looked me over and suggested what he wanted to do—I said yes to all of it. Soon, he had shaved my hair to less than one-half inch long and dyed my dark brown hair and eyebrows a beautiful red color. I was shocked when I saw the results in the mirror. The makeover truly changed my looks for the better.

SUCCESS AND STARVING

Next, my law clerk friend and I went to the makeup artist. He looked at her and said, "I will give you the expert treatment." He told me, "Honey, I'll go slow." He patiently taught me how to put makeup on. My mom did not wear makeup, and nobody had ever taught me how to wear it. I was thirty-three years old learning from a gay man how to use makeup to look professional.

For this job, I purchased a few more suits, still with the frugal mindset of buying a few high-quality suits instead of many cheaper things. Most of my clothes needed dry cleaning, but since I was such a rookie at wearing professional clothes, I didn't realize why they always came back from the cleaners with tin foil wrapped around the buttons. I had no idea that the dry cleaners protected the suit buttons that way, and I actually wore my jackets for several days with the foil still wrapped around the buttons. I did not realize my gaffe until some nice woman coached me in the ladies' restroom that I was supposed to remove the foil from my buttons. I felt so embarrassed.

Even though I was working in the city, riding public transportation, and rubbing shoulders with a multitude of DC professionals, I felt very out of place. I drew upon the strengths I learned growing up on the ranch: never stop until the work is done; work hard no matter what; and, it does not matter what others may think of me, it matters whether I show up and give my all to whatever project is in front of me. I took confidence in knowing that, even if I didn't know about taking the protective tinfoil off my buttons, I did know how to show up, be honest, and work hard.

While living in DC, I again lived in the church teaching center. When I was not working hard as a law clerk, I cleaned and cooked at the center. Also, I participated in morning, night, and weekend worship services, praying and asking God and the angels to help other people in their difficult lives.

During this second stint in DC, I became unable to work due to the severity of my pelvic pain. I had several surgeries, and the gynecologist was able to remove many of the endometrial cells that had migrated from the inside of my uterus to the external surfaces of the organs in my abdominal cavity. These surgeries provided me some relief, but this was the beginning of decades of pain.

After these surgeries, my doctor put me in touch with endometriosis support groups. Women who have endometriosis and have also had children say that the pain from endometriosis is as bad as childbirth pain. At one of these groups, I spoke with a nice woman who had suffered with endometriosis for years. She told me that she wished she had cancer because at least cancer would kill her. I decided this type of support was not helpful, and I did my best to power forward the only way I knew—by keeping myself in constant motion.

∞

CHAPTER 6

Powering through Pain

After my clerkship and for the next nineteen years, I enhanced my trauma superpower of being able to dissociate—in other words, leave my body and the pain—by developing strong concentration skills. After all, my clients needed me to focus on solving their problems. The competitive nature of litigation drove me further into sublimating my pain and personal needs so that I could prevail as an attorney. I cherished the role of being another's defender, and I found it easy to abandon myself to care for others.

Also, there were the practical drivers of the harsh world of being an associate attorney in law firms. At one of my first firm jobs, I came to a startling realization. When a new client called the front desk, whoever's name was next on the list was assigned to call the prospective client back. When it was my turn, I spent time with that person, heard their story, and determined a legal strategy or not. I kept track of my time as the firm charged the person for that time, and it seemed I was not supposed to care about the person even though they had just shared intimate parts of themselves. Charging by the hour, not allowing myself to care, and the revolving door of clients made me feel like I imagined a hooker might feel. I did not like this feeling.

I moved through five different associate attorney jobs over the next nineteen years throughout Montana, Washington, and Wyoming. I honed my skills at being an outer advocate while abandoning my inner self. My saving grace during this time was that one of the foals out of my beloved mare Jinx came back into my life. While I was working as the cow boss at the church's ranch, I had given Jinx to my friend Susan. I could not afford to pay for pasture, and Susan lived on a ranch where she could take care of Jinx, and she raised several of Jinx's foals.

One day my sister, Heidi, called and asked me if I wanted her to buy a horse for me from my mare Jinx. I told Heidi I was interested, and she drove to check this horse out. He was twelve years old at the time. My sister went to see and ride him and then called me. I asked what color he was, and she wasn't sure; he was an odd mix between a roan and a buckskin color with a black mane, a line down his back, and stripes around his legs. He was his own unique color. And with that, I bought him. Heidi and my parents visited me for my thirty-sixth birthday and delivered my new horse, a descendent of a 4-H project mare from all those years ago. I was so excited, waiting for my family to arrive and bring a horse into my life after more than ten years of being away from them.

When Heidi led him out of the trailer, he looked wild-eyed, like he was pretty wary of people. Even though I was so excited to have a horse again, I did not fall in love with him at first sight. He was a bit scary with his intense show of fearful reaction to his new surroundings. Yet, he was mine. I immediately started getting to know him. One of the first things I had to do was name him. Sometimes being an attorney is lonely because of the sacred duty of confidentiality, and I decided that I needed someone to talk to who would never repeat what I said. I named my horse Buddy, and he became my confidant.

Around that time, I had been working for a top litigation firm in Missoula, Montana. While there, I was recruited by one of their clients, the church ranch where I had been the cow boss years before. The Church Universal and Triumphant had an international presence, but its headquarters was in Gardiner, Montana, where its retreat center, Royal Teton Ranch, served members from around the world. The church recruited me to work as their in-house counsel because of my focus on land use issues and property rights. My job was to assist with nonprofit issues in addition to protecting the church's property rights. Also, like many churches and nonprofits, there was drama with internal politics, and I assisted the church in navigating that. Since my role as counsel meant that my main job and honorabe duty was to protect my client, the church, I did not have the luxury of sharing the information that people told me. I had the sacred, professional duties of confidentiality and privilege, which meant I could not emotionally process with others. I needed Buddy.

At first, our relationship was pretty rocky. Buddy did not trust me—or anyone else. I realized from how he was acting that he had been abused. All I knew about his history was that he had had several owners and had lived in various states in the Midwest before showing up in North Dakota. His then-owner found Heidi since our family name was on his Quarter Horse registration papers. Even though I had yet to deal with my own inner pain, I searched deep within myself to find ways to treat Buddy with compassion. Despite being a twelve-year-old gelding, his behavior was exasperating at times. He sometimes pulled back and broke things when tied. He did not trust me and often thought he knew better than I did. He was very much into self-preservation at all costs. In other words, he seemed to have a horse form of PTSD. When he pulled back and went a bit wild-eyed, he very much looked like he was suffering a flashback.

Outside of my still-steep climb as a developing lawyer, I spent a lot of time with Buddy. My heart was open and wanted to connect with him even though he often seemed emotionally unavailable. I was not very patient and had reactionary problems caused by my own PTSD, which I could not yet address. So I focused on developing a relationship with Buddy. After months of steady, compassionate treatment, Buddy started to warm toward me. We developed a respectful partnership and the ability to trust each other. He gradually let down his guard and moved toward me, and I fell in love with him.

One day after dealing with a particularly difficult legal issue at the church, I was riding and sharing my troubles with Buddy. I told him I was not going to trust or love people anymore because all they did was hurt me. Then, the strangest thing happened. Buddy told me, "I love you." I knew clearly in my heart that Buddy had spoken to me. Part of me was amused that my horse was nudging me forward on my spiritual path of opening my heart. Another part of me recoiled because I had never had a horse talk to me like this before. But within a nanosecond, I realized that Buddy was the obvious being to assist me. Indeed, he had overcome his fear and memories of abuse to open his heart to love and partner with me. My inner resistance started to melt. I realized that if the messenger is a horse, heed him.

The chronic pain that had engulfed me years before sometimes acted up when I was working or sitting in church services, praying or decreeing to help others in need across the world. In addition to the intense pelvic pain associated with endometriosis, I developed fibromyalgia and low back pain from my years of bending over to shoe horses. For me, the pain of fibromyalgia was like torture. I could feel the pain radiating from my bones to two to four inches on the outside of my feet, legs, arms, and hands. The pain felt like electric shocks blended with extremely sore muscles and bones. When the pain would become so bad that it interfered with my ability to focus, I could interrupt it by moving around. But as soon as my movement stopped, the pain would come back multiplied. There was sometimes nothing I could do to avoid the pain.

During one church service, the pain got so bad I could not focus on the prayers and decrees. Mother had been leading the service, but when I looked up to the altar, I noticed she was no longer there. An usher tapped me on the shoulder and whispered that Mother wanted to see me. He took me to a door beside the altar. I went through, and there was Mother. In outer life, she was much shorter and smaller than me. She walked up to me and put her arms around me. Her hug was so full of love, it seemed she was as big as an angel in the sky. Her love and her hug filled me with acceptance, love, and the belief that I was worthy. I surrendered to the love of the Divine Mother. To me, Mother was an open door to understanding attributes of a Mother that is beyond this realm. I realized that in my heart I had always loved the Divine Mother.

After receiving Mother's love and hug, I returned to my seat and realized that my once-frozen emotions were starting to flow. What was once only physical pain was also now an overwhelming emotional pain that I could not hold back. I did not want to break down sobbing in the middle of the service, so I decided to go home and rest. As I was leaving the church, Mother was at the back door. She reached out and hugged and held me again before I walked out. I do not remember either of us speaking any words. I did not realize it then, but I now know she and Buddy were both very important to my healing on multiple levels.

Even after my hugging encounter with Mother, my relationship with Buddy was a work-in-progress, and we sometimes butted heads. My internal world was topsy-turvy, and I reacted to Buddy like I had wanted to respond to my mom when I was five but hadn't out of fear. I got angry and scared, sometimes pulling Buddy's reins or lead rope, trying to force him to do what I wanted. Since he was also in recovery, he was stubborn and reacted to my requests in sometimes very strong, quick, scary ways. But he also provided me with the necessary balance I needed while striving to become a good attorney. We made slow but sure progress in our relationship, both of us learning to trust our hearts and move out of our trauma reactions.

Buddy and I moved to Olympia, Washington, for my next legal job, and the day after arriving, I remember trying to load him back into my two-horse trailer. Buddy hated that trailer. He had just ridden in it for thousands of miles, it was a tight fit for him, and it seemed he felt claustrophobic in there. On this very hot day in June, Buddy simply refused to load in the trailer. We fought for hours and were both drenched in sweat. I had used everything I knew to coerce him into the trailer. He reared, walked on his hind legs, pulled back, and did everything he could to refuse to load. Even though I was on the verge of losing my temper completely, I persevered, and he and I went head-to-head. I realized that even though he was battling me, he was also in control and was not going to hurt himself. This realization helped me keep on asking him to load. Finally, he backed down and got in the trailer. We were hours behind schedule to get to a ranch in

Eastern Washington where we were going to help move cows.

During the four-hour drive to our destination, I had to first recover from the three-hour physical and emotional battle. I needed water, food, and time to reestablish my inner harmony. I had been able to keep from totally losing myself in an angry reaction to Buddy, yet the battle was very emotional internally. A few hours later I was still pondering the conflict, and I realized that in the end, Buddy had joined my side of the battle. That was a big deal for him due to his past abuse. It seemed to me that he would now be watching me to see how I handled my victory. Would I lord it over him, or would I be gracious and move back into a partnership role? I decided that more than anything I wanted a trusting relationship with Buddy. So, for the next few days (and for the rest of his life), I was very devoted to letting him know that even though we battled, and I won that battle to load in the trailer, I valued his input and wanted to be his partner.

My new job in the state of Washington was serving as an attorney and lobbyist for the Washington Farm Bureau Federation. I worked on very important issues regarding agriculture and endangered salmon and bull trout as they related to numerous Native American tribes, four different states, and many different federal agencies. I was on a steep learning curve for the outer knowledge and skills to excel at my job. Buddy was a sweet spot in my life at that time.

Right before my fortieth birthday, I told my friend Kim, who trained horses and people for competitions, that I wanted to do a horseback riding event called "three-day eventing" on Buddy before the end of my fortieth year. When she realized that I was asking her to train me within the next year, she asked how old my horse was and whether he had ever jumped before. I told her Buddy was fourteen and that he had never jumped. Kim just rolled her eyes, but since she was a gutsy trainer, we started right away.

At one point, Kim decided she needed to ride Buddy because trying to train me to train Buddy was not really working. I warned her that Buddy had lots of stamina and that it was better to figure out how to encourage him to cooperate rather than fight with him because he could fight for a long time. They wound up in a battle and Kim found out the hard way that I was right. Somehow, they worked their way through the issue, and we began jumping.

When I first asked Buddy to jump over a cross rail, he seemed to say, *Why would I exert the energy to jump when I can walk around?* It was a valid question. Soon though, Buddy realized that he loved to jump. He was one of those horses that jumped with lots of force and a very round back—most often a foot over the height of the jump. He still was very much into self-preservation and was not going to let his feet touch whatever he was jumping. Consequently, he had a very good jumping style with his front knees picked as high up as he could get them.

Within eight months, Buddy and I entered our first three-day event. The first event was dressage, which is a kind of horse dancing. Buddy and I had to maintain a connection and specific style while changing direction and pace. We did fine, even though I almost forgot the pattern of our test.

The next event was cross-country jumping. Both Buddy and I loved this part of the competition the most. For more than ten minutes we jumped around a course of up to three-foot jumps. After the first jump, he took an extra hop to show his happiness. We were a team, and I'll never forget the feeling of total oneness.

The last event was stadium jumping. While I was warming up for stadium jumping, I got nervous, and Kim realized that I was passing that on to Buddy, so she told me to get off and hold him. Our first round was a little wild because I came from a rodeo background and Buddy was all too happy to go fast, but speed was not the point of the stadium jumping. Still, we did well enough to win a ribbon at the three-day event.

After this competition, Buddy and I were united. Together we had overcome reacting to each of our underlying PTSD and each other's responses. We learned to trust each other and jump obstacles in places we had never been before.

Even though I was riding again and enjoying my partnership with Buddy, the pain in my physical body escalated to an unbearable level while I was living and working in Washington. I had severe endometriosis and had undergone surgery five times by then. Also, in addition to the fibromyalgia and the low back pain from my horseshoeing and my rodeoing days, I now started suffering from migraine headaches at least once per week. To make matters worse, the constant stress seemed to heighten my pain. After borrowing money to pay for college and law school and then having health problems, I never had enough money to make ends meet. I was very concerned about being able to pay my bills, and I often resorted to payday loans to pay my bills on time.

One day when I was driving home from work, my dad called me and, during the conversation, casually dropped that he had lymphoma and that the cancer was in his bones. I had to stop my car and ask him to repeat himself. After he started chemo, I took time off and drove home to help my mom take care of him. I stayed with them for several weeks in Montana before returning to my job in Washington.

One day at work, the pressure of living with horrible pain in my body, striving to be professional, and worrying about money and my dad all got to be too much. I was unable to function and ended up in the emergency room. The doctors checked me out and gave me painkillers to get me through the crisis. I knew that going to the emergency room would not offer me any long-term solutions for my escalating chronic pain. I then found the best gynecologist that I could, made an appointment, marched into her office, and asked if she would remove my uterus and ovaries. She told me that because I had already had so many surgeries, she thought another one would only create more scar tissue and exacerbate the pain. She refused to perform the surgery and suggested that I take narcotic pain medication and an antidepressant and do physical therapy. I questioned her about taking narcotics, because of my mom's history as an alcoholic. I knew that it was highly likely that I had an addictive personality. In the end, I decided to trust her and took the pills.

I realized that I was no longer tough enough to deal with my emotional pain either. I called the doctor back and asked her for a referral to a psychological counselor. The doctor told me that my pain might stay with me for the rest of my life. Since I realized that my pain may never go away, I decided I needed help changing my reaction to the severe pain that had become intolerable at many levels of my being. She referred me to Dr. Donna Lidren, and I started therapy.

Going to see Dr. Lidren was very hard for me to do. Even though I was a successful professional adult, my childhood trauma had hijacked all my feelings. I recognized that part of me wanted to connect with Dr. Lidren and trust her. At some level, there was nothing I wanted more in the world than to find a safe relationship within which to heal. But another part of me was triggered, terrified, and on the verge of running away from therapy or any kind of relationship with her. I could see her inner tomboy child shining through her professional veneer, which appealed to my own inner tomboy. Dr. Lidren was very kind, and since she was younger than me, I did not completely project my mom onto her. She was able to help me learn to "stay in the boat" no matter what. This meant that I wouldn't cave into my unconscious need to move away from a relationship with her.

Somehow in our sessions, Dr. Lidren was able to keep me from running from a connection with her. She taught me to overcome the defenses I had created in childhood to survive my mom's tirades and abuse. In my relationship with her, I had my second experience, after Mother hugging and loving me, of being in a healing, supportive relationship. Dr. Lidren taught me the foundation of understanding myself and how to be in a relationship with someone who had my best interests at heart. She shared her patience and support with me and helped me find the resources to take baby steps forward out of my PTSD response to life.

After several years in Washington, I was sitting at my desk in my small office cubicle at the Washington Farm Bureau, and I answered my phone. The caller asked, "This is the White House, may I speak with Hertha Lund?" My initial response was that someone was pulling a prank on me, but I wasn't sure, so I answered that this was Hertha. The caller proceeded to inform me that the White House was inquiring to see if I was interested in taking a position in the Bush Administration at the United States Department of the Interior or the Environmental Protection Agency. I was flattered by the call, but part of me did not want to move back to Washington, DC for a third tour. But, instead of sharing my reluctance, I answered as any ambitious attorney who works in the policy arena should and told the caller I was interested.

After several months of phone discussions, a series of interviews in DC, and much soul-searching, I decided that I did not feel inspired to take a job in DC again—even if it was the White House asking. By that time, I had Buddy, a dog named Sam, and a pet rabbit. Try as I might, I could not imagine a scenario where I could fit my current lifestyle into living in DC. I simply could not make myself go back to only living for my professional development and not being able to spend time with Buddy and my other pet friends. Taking the job would mean not only having no time to spend with Buddy but also not being able to afford to board him where I could go and say an occasional hello. As much as I tried to find a way forward that included both accepting the honor of serving the president as well as having time in my life for what I loved outside of my professional career, I couldn't. I turned down the opportunity.

While making that difficult decision, I called an attorney who had been my mentor, and she, sensing my need for a change while keeping a balance, recruited me to work for her in Cheyenne, Wyoming. I accepted, and Kim and Heidi helped me move my menagerie of animal friends from Washington to Wyoming. Cheyenne is located on the prairie at an altitude of 6,063 feet. The wind seemed to blow continuously, and the winters could be harsh. I loved my job and the people I worked with, but I did not love living in Cheyenne.

During my three years there, I focused on continuing to develop my professional skills in litigation. The law firm I worked for litigated cases across the West on behalf of farmers, ranchers, and other landowners. I learned that law is called a "practice" for a reason. It requires lots of it to develop the needed understanding, skills, and abilities to provide good legal representation in courtroom scenarios. My boss was a very good example, and I made progress. However, I often felt impatient, as I didn't think my career progress was good or fast enough.

At this time, I was still engaged in my daily spiritual practice and serving my church in leadership positions on the board of directors and the council of elders. Since I had the dual outer focuses of developing my trial and legal skills and serving as a leader in my spiritual community, my inner focus was lacking. I used the outer focus to help me avoid my inner pain. I resumed disassociating to avoid feeling my unresolved pain and tried to focus solely on my outer challenges, which were more than adequate to consume all my energy. My outer striving and focus allowed me to ignore the emotional and ever-growing physical pain lodged in my body. I continued to strengthen my superpower to ignore it and concentrate on everything else.

During this time in the wilderness of the high Wyoming plains, I met my future husband. I was in my early forties and had had many conversations with God about my desire to meet a man with whom to share my life. Since these prayers seemed to go unanswered, I had surrendered and told God that I would not look right or left—if I were destined to meet the man of my life, God would have to dance him across my desk. While John did not literally dance across my desk, his case did.

Since I was licensed in Montana, the law firm assigned me a case from Montana in which three different ranches were litigating with the United States Forest Service regarding the rules governing grazing on federal lands. The landowners worked as a team in partnering with me and others at the law firm to represent their interests. Before a big litigation deadline, the ranchers flew me to Montana to meet with them because it was cheaper to pay for my travel to come to them than it was for all of them to travel to Cheyenne to meet with me. While I was in Montana, staying at one of the ranch manager's houses for a dinner meeting with the landowners, I asked the hostess whose wife or mother had cooked the main dish. My host answered that John, one of the ranchers, had made the dish himself.

Part of me wanted to quip, "Where has he been all my life—a rancher who cooks?" A voice in my head said, *He is the one*, very loud and clear. This whole inner conversation kind of scared me. I decided not to say any smart-ass comments out loud and instead just waited to see what would unfold.

At that time, besides working with him to edit briefs and strategize moving the legal case forward, I had paid very little attention to John. I could pick his strong, distinct voice out in a crowd, but I could not have told you whether his hair was blond or black or any other identifying features. I was very disciplined at not looking at my clients as potential relationship material. I was very sincere about following the code of ethics and only had my client's best interest in mind.

This case, as many do, went on for several years. During this time, my dad died in Montana, and I went home for several weeks for the funeral and to help my mom. John heard about my dad dying, and this is when our professional relationship deepened into a friendship. We talked often regarding the litigation, and on one of these calls, I shared with him my sorrow and pain about losing my dad. I was a daddy's girl. John compassionately asked me what he could do to help, offering to come to the funeral and sit beside me during the service. I accepted his support.

Sometime in the next year, I argued the ranchers' case before the federal district court in Helena, Montana, after many meetings with my rancher clients, including John. I lost the case, but we appealed to the Ninth Circuit Court of Appeals based on the district court's errors. While the case was on appeal, my clients settled the case. So I no longer served as the ranchers' attorney, and I no longer had a professional relationship with John.

As often happened, when my inner compass prompted me to move onward on my life path, I felt uncomfortable. This time, my inner push was enhanced because I was hopeful that my relationship with John would turn into something more. As usual, my feelings of terror and fear surfaced in waves, with the additional fear that my hopes for a loving relationship would be dashed. I resorted to prayer and asked for spiritual guidance. My prompting was to search for a legal job in Montana. In keeping with my usual pattern, I was recruited to work for a small firm in Bozeman, Montana. I had several interviews and found my next job as an attorney.

Upon returning to Montana, I rented a house near Bozeman and started my twelfth year of practicing law. Somewhere around that time, I read the book *Outliers* by author Malcolm Gladwell. In it, he wrote that it takes at least ten thousand hours to become proficient at mastering any task, whether it be playing hockey, playing cello, or a profession.[2] I had certainly practiced law for more than ten thousand hours by this time and had taken my sixth job as an attorney. However, I was still striving for excellence, fueled by the twin fires of fear of failure and my inner desire to fulfill my reason for being.

Several months after I moved back to Montana, John asked me out on our first date. We had become good friends by then, and looking back, since we were both a bit old-fashioned in our approach to dating, it was fortunate that we had met and were first protected from the pressures of dating because of our professional relationship. We discovered that we had more than a friendship growing between us and dated for several years before we were married.

During this time, I put down roots for the first time and borrowed money from John to build a house in Bozeman. My job at the small firm was stressful because I did not always see eye to eye with my boss. We differed in our approaches to taking care of our clients' interests as well as in the business aspect—who made how much money. Even though I still wore my outer persona of being tougher than nails, I often cried when we went through the bills. Part of me hated charging my clients so much money to fight against those who had wronged them. Even worse than that, my boss was subjective in how much he paid me each month. So I never knew whether I would make enough to cover my bills. I no longer used payday loans to get from paycheck to paycheck, but money was still an issue for me.

On the good side of life's ledger, I had two horses and kept them at a boarding facility near where I lived. I was able to ride often and spent many hours with Buddy. Sometimes, Buddy and I would travel to John's ranch and help him with ranch work. I loved visiting him and being able to be involved with ranching again.

For me, it seemed like John and I had dated forever. I was in my mid-forties and certainly felt my biological clock ticking. Also, I was acutely aware that John was the youngest and only boy in his family, which meant that it was logical that his children, if he ever had any, would be heirs to the family ranch. John's family ranch, the Grande Ranch, was established after John's great-grandfather immigrated from Norway in 1877. This was prior to Montana becoming a state and only one year after Custer's Last Stand. The heritage of the Grande Ranch and my concerns about having children after so many surgeries for endometriosis were on a collision course.

During the years we dated, we discussed several times whether we wanted children, and I was candid with him that if he did, I was probably not the right person to marry. Somehow, we made it through these hard conversations. Before getting married, we counseled with a local Lutheran minister. During that process, the pastor asked us to think ahead to our fiftieth wedding anniversary and see who might attend our party and what we would serve them. I jokingly answered that since we were in our mid-forties, we would invite any of our friends who were still alive and serve them apple sauce since we would be more than ninety-five.

The pastor also asked John why he was marrying me, because I was not going to stay home, cook his meals, and clean the house. I imagine he asked John this question because the local ranching community is pretty traditional, and the pastor wanted to make sure we were both ready for my nontraditional role of being a professional who was unwilling to drop her career to be a rancher's wife. John answered that he was happy that I had my professional life and that we would figure out a way to make our lives work together. The pastor did ask me how I thought we would deal with the fact that my legal office was in Bozeman, which is more than ninety miles from the ranch. I replied that we would do the best we could to make it work, and John responded that at least we would be trying to find time to spend together instead of trying to find time to be separate, as some married couples did.

After John asked me to marry him, I said yes and told him that it was fine with me if we just got married in a church with both of our mothers in attendance. No part of me wanted a large wedding. The thought of all those people looking at me in a dress was almost unbearable. I was also worried as I did not have any money to pay for a wedding, and neither did my mom. I did not want John to have to pay what my family was traditionally supposed to pay. He responded that he had family, friends, and neighbors that he would like to invite to our wedding. So we had the wedding at John's family ranch on a beautiful spring day, and we both loved the experience. We chose to share our love of each other and God with all those who came to celebrate with us.

The first few years of our marriage felt like the honeymoon period, but I still had some insecurities. Since high school, I had never lived more than two or three years in one place. Even though I loved working on John's ranch, I tried to avoid falling in love with the land. My pain from losing our family ranch was still too great to risk loving someone else's land. Today, the ranch that was my husband's and his family's land is still my home, but back then, it felt risky to relax into the fortunate circumstances of being married to and loved by a ranching man.

Neither John nor I had been married before, and I was so happy to find the man of my dreams, even if later than I had hoped. At some level, I believed that getting married, being loved, and having a secure home would cause my inner pain to disappear. But that did not happen. Instead, marrying John and being loved by him put my inner unresolved pain on steroids and forced the pain to the surface. One time we were arguing in a minor way, and I fell into the well of my unresolved childhood pain. I said something about being scared. He asked me what I was scared about. In my mind's eye, I saw someone with their hands around my neck, tossing me away. I answered that I was afraid he would throw me away. He looked me in the eye, his features softening in compassion and his eyes watering. He told me he would never throw me away. I succumbed to feeling the deep, inner pain and cryed without understanding where it was coming from.

Early on in our marriage, I understood fully that John loved me for who I was and that he was there to support me to the best of his ability. This was the first time I believed I was loved in my life. I knew I loved him, yet I still sometimes felt unworthy and untrusting of his, or even God's, love.

Both John and I spent long hours on our respective businesses. He spent his time working on and managing the ranch, and I spent my time on my law practice. I opened my own practice, Lund Law, the year after we were married. We were both busy, and we both liked to work. Occasionally, we traveled together to attend seminars related to one of our jobs or took vacations to someplace on a large body of water. John loves to vacation near the water—and I love John.

I still lived in the shadow of immense pain, but focusing on work helped me to stave off what I was sure would kill me if I allowed myself to feel it. Six years into our marriage, I started falling apart on multiple levels. Several decades of long hours, litigating or negotiating for my clients on a variety of issues caught up with me. My unresolved stuff surfaced from the dark recesses of my being because I was stretched so thin at all levels and because I felt loved, supported, and safe with John. Allowing love in drove the pain out of the deep caverns and recesses of my heart where I had tried to bury it.

Until marrying John, I always craved intimacy and wanted to be in a relationship, but I often ran away from others if they got too close. I did not want to get hurt. My drive to get away was underneath my awareness, yet it was so compelling that I often felt like escape was the only way to survive. But my game face was practiced, and I doubt many of my friends or early boyfriends realized that my strategy was to run if anybody got too close.

I now know that running away amplified the wound created by my experiences with my mom and the sexual abuse in childhood. John loved me so much that one time, when we were in a heated disagreement and I was getting ready to run away from the house, he put his arms around me and held me. Sometimes that's what it took.

John's love was fundamental and foundational for my path to healing. I once again also had heaven on Earth because I brought several of my horses, including my beloved Buddy, to live with us at the ranch. I had the best life I could on the outer, but I still had inner pain that followed me wherever I went, emerging in worse ways than ever before. Feeling safe opened the floodgates, forcing me to feel the pain I ran from feeling before.

CHAPTER 7

Dying to Live

∞

Six years into our marriage, I hit rock bottom on all levels of being. My chest started hurting and just got worse. I spent lots of time visiting doctors and going in and out of the emergency room.

One morning, I decided not to go to work because my chest was hurting so badly. I stayed home and then around 10:00 a.m., I decided to try to go to work. While in the car, I realized I was in no condition to drive or work and turned around. Once I arrived home, I realized that something was really wrong and called 911. They told me to take an aspirin, unlock the door, and lie down if I felt like I needed to. Soon the paramedics arrived. They had a very hard time inserting an IV into my arm because my blood pressure had dropped very low from the pain. Finally, after several attempts, they were able to get an IV in and then they loaded me up in the ambulance.

Upon arriving at the emergency room, I was surrounded by many doctors and nurses because, based on my symptoms, they thought I was having some type of cardiac event. They hooked me up to multiple monitors, took blood, did an EKG, and sent me for further testing. To do the heart imaging to determine whether one of my heart valves was malfunctioning or had ruptured, they needed to insert contrast, which required a second IV. To insert a second IV, they needed to do an ultrasound, and so an ultrasound machine needed to be tracked down. And that is how, even though I was in the emergency room for suspected heart issues, somehow, I was left, forgotten, unattended, and unmonitored while someone searched for the ultrasound. I remember lying on the gurney by myself, scared that I was dying, all alone for what seemed like hours but probably was more like a half hour. I had the very scary realization that I may not be safe depending on them to help me.

After the ultrasound and other tests, the doctors diagnosed pericarditis—inflammation in the membrane sac around my heart. Even though pericarditis can be very painful, it usually isn't fatal. So, though the doctor had previously told me they were going to keep me overnight to monitor me, he now told me they were going to send me home. I asked him how I would get home since I rode there in the ambulance. He said they would call me a cab. I mentioned that I was worried about being able to walk to the door. He said they could take me in a wheelchair. I felt scared of dying and being abandoned by those who were paid to care for me.

After that episode, I was in and out of the ER for ongoing bouts of pericarditis. I consulted with experts, but no doctor could tell me what was causing the pericarditis or what we might do to treat the inflammation around my heart. Looking back, it makes perfect sense that my physical heart suffered from inflammation because emotionally, I was suffering from many heartaches in my life.

The pain in my chest kept getting progressively worse over the year. By fall, when John and I would walk to watch our nephew play college football, he would have to walk slowly because I did not have enough oxygen to walk at a normal speed. The pain, which felt like a rectangular box around my heart, was worse at night when I was lying down, so I started sleeping in a recliner because the pain was somewhat better when I was on an incline.

Sometime in November, the pain was so bad one night that I decided I wanted John to take me to the hospital in Billings. I had lost faith in the hospital in Bozeman—they had failed to diagnose and treat me effectively. I remember that I was sitting in the recliner in the living room at 3:00 a.m., and I decided I could wait for John to get up at five to tell him I wanted him to take me to the hospital. Waiting was probably not a very good decision, but I did not want to disrupt John's sleep.

When he got up, I asked him to please drive me to the Billings hospital. He said he would do chores and then we could go. I told him no, I need to go now, and that I was scared that I would not make it if we waited any longer. We both got dressed and got on the road. During the drive, the vibrations from the road were causing me unbearable pain, and I was moaning while John was driving. He had never heard me moan before. Neither had I. I had a habit of being amazingly stoic—the more pain I had, the flatter my affect became.

We had to go through Harlowton, Montana, on the way to Billings. I felt so bad that I did not know if I could stand the trip to Billings. I had been to the ER in Harlowton before, and I knew that the hospital had a helipad to transport emergency patients to Billings. I asked John if he would stop at Harlowton so they could help me.

In what seemed like a miracle, I was taken care of in the ER by a doctor who specialized in heart medicine and was serving as the main doctor for the Harlowton clinic and ER. She had great credentials and knew what she was doing. She did her tests and diagnosed me with pericarditis and pneumonia. I had been in the Bozeman hospital one day before, and they had failed to diagnose pneumonia. The doctor put a heart monitor on me and asked if I wanted to stay there under her care or go on to Billings. I decided that I felt safe with her, and I stayed in one of the few patient rooms for several days.

Within one week of my return home from the Harlowton clinic, I received a call that my mom had fallen and was unconscious. John and I got in the car and drove to Lewistown, where mom had been living, and went to the hospital where my family had gathered. Mom was still alive when we arrived. I sat by my mom's side as we surrounded her in the hospital bed. I told her it was okay for her to leave her body. I told her I loved her and thanked her for giving me life. She made her transition with very little effort. For the next few weeks after my mom passed, the heart doctor continued to try to diagnose and treat what was going on in my chest. After she had exhausted what she could do from Harlowton, she referred me to a heart specialist in Billings. John and I traveled to Billings the night before my appointment because there was a huge winter storm, and my appointment was early in the morning. Again, the vibrations from the road caused me to feel unbearable pain. I did my best to keep quiet because John was having enough difficulty with the icy roads and blizzard conditions.

Sometime in the middle of the night, I was lying awake at the hotel and realized that something else was wrong. I took note of my symptoms and how I felt, and I realized that I might be getting septic. My inner prompting was that I was seriously sick, and I needed medical help. My appointment with the heart specialist was first thing in the morning, so when we got there and the nurse came in to hook me up, I told her that I wanted the doctor to call ahead and ask them to admit me to the hospital through the ER. She went to get the doctor. He came in, listened to me tell him how bad I felt, listened to my heart, reviewed the EKG, and said he wanted me to go to the ER.

Once I was in the ER, I met my hospitalist doctor. He ran more tests and found out that my CRP, which is a measure of inflammation in the body, was 187. Usually, if someone has a CRP over three, the doctors get concerned. The hospitalist wanted me to take steroids. Even though I was in such pain, I still had my wits about me, and I argued with him. I had taken steroids before, and I did not like how they impacted me. Also, I knew that nobody was certain if my problems were being caused by an infection or something else. Having studied medicine, I knew that using steroids if I had an infection could be catastrophic. I won that round with the hospitalist.

Several doctors met in my hospital room with me to try to determine what they might do to help me stay alive. All the testing revealed high inflammation, yet none of them knew the cause. I had the best lung doctor, the best heart doctor, a very good hospitalist, an infectious disease expert, and a surgeon all brainstorming to help me. They included me in this process because I had been a pre-med student, I was cognizant of my history and important anomalies in my health, and even though I was in a lot of pain, I was able to stay present and troubleshoot with them.

After a whole new battery of tests, my diagnosis was pericarditis, pneumonia, and pleurisy for unknown reasons. In other words, I had severe inflammation and fluid around my heart and lungs, but nobody knew what was causing it. Upon admission, one of the first procedures they did was to remove 600 ml of fluid from around my left lung. They also ran tests to check me for every infection that they thought I might have been exposed to living in rural Montana on a ranch, including brucellosis.

In December 2015, less than one month after my mom died at the age of eighty-eight, I found myself talking to God while breathing oxygen through tubes. I wasn't in the ICU, but I was not on a regular floor either. Other patients on my floor had lung and heart problems. I was aware that several of the patients neighboring my room coded and passed on from their bodies while I was there.

I knew I, too, might soon leave my body. I pondered this and realized that part of me did not want to live on Earth anymore. For sure, this was not my home and God must have screwed up. I still hurt from my childhood wounds. I never felt like I fit in. All my life I had a hard time dealing with the cruelness I experienced from other people. I was not scared of dying and wanted to go home to God.

I thought of what I loved about life on Earth. I loved my husband, my dogs, my horses, my spiritual community, and many others. Yet, when I talked to God, I was at the point of deciding that all those I loved could get by without me. I was ready to leave this place that part of me believed was not my home. I felt that I was leaving and moving up out of my body, and I thought, *Soon, I will see God.* I was so excited. I felt a light warmth and sense of being home beyond anything I had experienced in my human body. At that moment, I felt swaddled in the love of the Divine Mother, the angels, and all of God's creation. No part of my being was separated from the all-encompassing feeling of oneness with soft, warm safety and the total absence of anything less than love and light. Then, it dawned on me that God was not going to be happy to see me because I was not done. My reason for being was not completed. I realized that I wanted to fulfill my reason for being no matter the cost.

I suddenly did not feel so jubilant and realized I did not have much time to come up with a way to stop my rising out of my body into the light. I had to find a way to continue to live. I looked down at my body—I did not want to get back in it. I had extreme systemic inflammation throughout my whole body, but most severely around my heart and lungs. My body hurt so badly all over that even my teeth fillings hurt. But the pain in my body was the tip of the iceberg—underneath all the physical pain was my deep unresolved pain from my childhood wounds. I went deep within, and I promised God that I would do whatever it took to get into my body and become whole.

My promise worked. I moved away from the freedom and great sense of love and light that I had felt while leaving my body and moving toward reunion with God. Instead of continuing to move up and out, I got back into my heavy, painful, damaged body and started doing whatever it took to become whole. Part of me would have rather crawled into a road-killed elk carcass on the highway than get back into my body.

I spent a total of six days in the hospital, from December 17 to December 23, 2015. On the fourth day of being hospitalized, the surgeon did exploratory surgery and biopsied material from my left lung. The team of doctors did not find the cause of the severe inflammation in my body that had almost led to my leaving my body and this life. But even though it seemed the good doctors had not solved my health problems, I left the hospital with a new zeal for living and the determination to do whatever it took to heal.

I wished I could tell you that from that point on everything got better, that my body no longer hurt, that I no longer struggled to breathe, that the medical doctors eventually pinpointed what was going wrong in my body, and that they prescribed a treatment that was right on point. I wish I could tell you that I miraculously healed with the help of modern medicine. But it was months, even years, before I started feeling comfortable living in my body.

Since I had ignored the deep emotional pain for so long, the trauma had impacted my physical body, and I exhibited almost all the problems that Kelly McDaniel writes about in her book *Mother Hunger*. In her book, she stated that if as a child "essential elements of maternal nurturance and protection were missing, you didn't stop loving your mother, you simply didn't learn to love yourself."[3] Also, she explained that the worse form of Mother Hunger is complex PTSD. She said, "As adults, women with Third-Degree Mother Hunger, the term that is used to describe those with complex PTSD, often suffer physical symptoms of trauma. Physical symptoms may include back pain and neck pain, fibromyalgia, migraines, spastic colon or irritable bowel syndrome, allergies, thyroid and other endocrine disorders, chronic fatigue, and some forms of asthma."[4] Prior to my near-death, I experienced and was medically treated for all of these physical symptoms. When I left the hospital, I found the will and desire to live, but I had a deep well of disease in my body and being that I needed to work through. At that time, I did not realize that I had Third-Degree Mother Hunger.

∞

Part II

CHAPTER 8

Heal Thyself

∞

The morning after my talk with God and being granted more time in my physical body to complete my purpose for this life, I pondered what the right next step was to honor my promise. I surveyed where I was and realized that I had good doctors and healthcare—and that neither of those would heal me. No doubt the care I received helped me stay alive and make it through my health crisis. Yet they had no clue what was causing the extraordinarily high inflammation around my heart and lungs and throughout my body. I realized that I could not count on the doctors to heal whatever was at the core of my health problems.

This is when I took my most important step toward wholeness. I accepted responsibility for my condition and trusted God, the light, his emissaries, and the angels to lead me to healing. But I knew the responsibility was mine to move forward where directed and to do the hard inner work that would be required to heal myself at multiple levels of being. This is when I started a true inner walk toward finding my oneness with the Divine. Certainly, at times I was scared and had doubt and fear, as my previous choices in this life had not always been that great at leading me toward wholeness. However, I knew that this was my inner mountain to climb, and I moved forward in faith.

As I was getting very real with myself, even though my physical body was so sick, it seemed I had extra access to other parts of myself. I found inner resources that I had heretofore ignored. These resources and resilience were created and installed early in my life as a response to the trauma from my childhood. I used every ounce of knowledge, awareness, self-mastery, and resources I had to anchor me.

I pondered what I remembered spiritually about healing from the thirty years I had studied spiritual teachings with Mother at the Summit Lighthouse. In addition to learning about spiritual healing, I had also been a pre-med and pre-vet student with a passion for healing at all levels of being. I also knew that invoking light through prayer and meditation would help me enter the heart of God. I remembered the healing thoughtform, which is three concentric spheres: green on the outside, blue in the middle, and white at the center. At the core of this thoughtform is the fiery white that symbolizes purity. Next, there is the blue sheath of light that denotes the will of God. The outer sphere is a mighty vibrating sheath of healing green light. If I could visualize and feel these spheres around my being, body, heart, and lungs, I could assist in my healing at the soul level and the healing of my organs, cells, and tissues in my physical body.

Also, I remembered how important it was for my healing to use my throat chakra to invoke light by saying prayers and mantras out loud. So I again practiced the science of the spoken word by saying mantras that vibrated congruent with the violet flame. I also remembered how much better I felt when I prayed the rosary to Mother Mary.

Even though I looked inward for healing, I knew that I was very sick and that I would need to keep open to outer healing to receive that specific alchemical formula of inner and outer healing. I had left the hospital several days before Christmas armed with follow-up appointments with my heart and lung doctors, a referral to a naturopathic doctor who might be able to help address my conditions, a promise to God to do whatever it took to heal, and my inner awareness that I alone was responsible for my healing.

This whole process humbled me to my core. I was not in charge, and I could not control anything. Even though I had been successful at multiple levels of life before my near-leaving embodiment episode, my success did not entitle me to be in control.

I do not like calling leaving my body experience a near-death experience (NDE). To me, it was gaining a new awareness of life or a rebirth experience. I realized that I had been living as if I were partially dead. By that I mean, on multiple levels, I was shut off from being totally alive. I did not actively ever choose a suicide attempt, yet my way of living meant dying a bit daily, or, in other words, committing suicide slowly, without leaving fingerprints. I restricted myself from being alive in the here and now because I still carried a heavy load from my past, and I feared the future.

In my spiritual studies, I read that what I fear most becomes my God, a false God. Also, I read that before experiencing freedom, deep peace, and wholeness, I had to face and conquer the fear of death. Based on my experience of ascending up and out of my body, I realized that my previous understanding of death was all wrong. When I was out of my body, I did not think about how much I had worked, how hard I strived to get ahead in life, how much money I made, or how many legal cases I had won or lost. Instead, when I was between here and there, I thought about who I loved, what I loved, and whether I had accomplished my purpose for being born. After that experience, I was no longer afraid of "dying"—but I was afraid of not living. To the new me, dying was not any more emotional than trading in my pickup or other vehicle for a new one. I drove that vehicle for a long time and have had some interesting—and maybe some not-so-interesting—experiences in it. I would continue my journey and experiences in a new vehicle. To me, "dying" is now more like changing my address of where I exist in my service to God than it is the end of my existence.

Soon after leaving the hospital and embarking on fulfilling my promise to God, I decided to run for political office as well as to take a stand in my church community. Neither of these decisions made sense based on how sick I was. I knew I was still quite ill, yet I was inwardly driven to take both of these actions. Until this time, I had been in harmony with church leadership and, in fact, had served multiple years in leadership. When, more recently, I was asked to give my professional opinion about several issues though, my input was not received well by those in leadership at that time.

One of my friends in the leadership of the church told me that if I pursued taking a stand in opposition to the leaders, I would get hurt. But I believed in the spiritual teachings of love, honor, and wisdom upon which the church was founded. So, I took the hard path forward.

Looking back now, it seems parts of me still had to die further. After dying, I was even more determined than ever to listen to the still, small voice within, even though it did not really make sense to me or those around me.

Throughout my youth, I always sought leadership positions in every organization I was part of. I studied leadership skills with 4-H and FFA and once even traveled to Washington, DC for a weeklong leadership training. I first started public speaking in contests when I was nine years old and always saw myself serving as a leader in my community.

After working at several state legislatures and the United States Congress as a journalist and lobbyist, I thought I had much to offer my local community, so I signed up to run for the state Senate when a seat opened up. Immediately, I ran into resistance. John was not very supportive, and I was naive about how running would stir up prejudice about my religious path. Throughout the whole race, John stood back, and though he wanted to love and support me, I could see his pain from witnessing how people treated me.

My political race was most active from January to June, starting just weeks after I had been released from the hospital. Many days I still had trouble breathing and did not have the energy to do much at all, much less campaign for public office. Still, I tried to get myself out to meet people, make phone calls, and do the things necessary for my campaign. By winter's end, I had several people help put up signs and held some meetings with potential voters throughout the district's hundreds of square miles. I felt like my communication skills were serving me well in getting my message out there.

Then, one day, cruel reality hit. I was in a bar in a small local town giving a speech to potential voters. (In rural Montana the most common place for people to gather socially is a bar.) At the end of my talk, a man said he wanted to ask me a question in private. I replied that he could ask me in front of all those gathered. Internally, I thought

I might as well address his concerns in public because I was sure he was already talking publicly about whatever he was going to ask me.

He told me he was a believer in Jesus and read the Bible. I said I was too. He shot back, "No you are not." He went on to call me a "cult member." I asked him, "Who made you the Taliban of Christianity?" The entire exchange was very harsh. I felt judged, condemned, and all alone. I pointed out to him the irony of his treatment of me while at the same time claiming his own Christianity.

Later in the race, a few days before the election, a local rancher took out a quarter-page newspaper ad in which he called me "a fraud, a Democrat, and a cult leader." Prior to this, others had dabbled in saying means things about me in the press. Since I was trained to spin and had fought at the Washington DC–level of politics, my impulse was to use my skills and blister my opponent. But John told me, "If you fight with a pig, you both get dirty, and the pig likes it." I told him, "I'll like it too," but I listened to John—I did not deploy my skills and lose my soul.

I lost the race. I won a respectable number of votes, and I won in my home county. Still, I felt devastated. I had not lost at anything in life this badly before. I did not have many skills for coping with failure. I was a little miffed at John for not supporting me more during the race, but I was grateful for his kind, gentle support as I recovered from a very public defeat and a beating from the press.

At the same time that I was being publicly ridiculed for my membership in a non-mainstream church, some in my church community also rejected me. I had served the church as an elder and as a member of the board of directors for almost fifteen years and had become the go-to person to interpret the church's articles of incorporation. Some of the elders were concerned about how the executive branch of the church was implementing their direction, and they asked me if I thought these actions were in alignment with the articles. Since I had been in leadership and was being asked by elders, who had the duty to protect the church, I answered honestly, making my written response available to all the elders.

Apparently, many of those in leadership positions in the church did not like my response and decided to try to destroy my good name in the church community. Some of the leaders mounted a campaign to spread mistruths about me. This was especially painful because the teachings of the church are about honor and love. By that time, I had given more than thirty years to serving the church in various roles. I thought it was my home away from home. I felt so betrayed, so hurt and sad that those who served in leadership of the church would misuse their positions of power to hurt me. My soul further withered up and died inside me. I went deeper within, relying upon God instead of humans. Also, since I felt so wounded by the leadership's actions, in reaction I wrote some things that I wished I had not written.

I was still reeling from my leaving of this realm and returning to my body and climbing out of the deep hole of physical disease. I was unbalanced because I had given up my old, avoidant ways of dealing with pain. If I had not died and made my promise to God, I am pretty sure that I would not have had the grit and resilience to continue on at this time. Other than John remaining by my side, I felt so rejected. I felt like day was night and that there was no light. Within, I felt dry, damaged, and totally alone. I wanted to stop moving forward on my inner climb—my life seemed unworthy of the effort.

Childhood memories of being abandoned and rejected surfaced, leaving me highly inflamed and with unbearable pain. First, I felt that my mom did not love me. Now, I felt my local community and my church did not love or want me. As in my childhood, I felt like there was no place for me to find safety and peace to be me. I lost my ability to stay grounded in my desire to do no harm to others. There were times when I wanted to make those who were hurting me also feel pain.

I wanted to use my communication skills to fight back against those whom I felt were treating me unfairly. John and some close friends helped me to not act with vengeance, meanness, or darkness against those who were hurting me. Instead of fighting back, I chose to go within and seek connection to God and continue to heal what was still not whole inside me.

Dark Night of the Soul

On a dark night, Kindled in love with yearnings—oh, happy chance?—
I went forth without being observed, My house being now at rest.

In darkness and secure, By the secret ladder, disguised—oh, happy chance!—
In darkness and in concealment, My house being now at rest.

In the happy night, In secret, when none saw me,
Nor I beheld aught, Without light or guide, save that which burned in my heart.

The light guided me More surely than the light of noonday
To the place where he (well I knew who!) was awaiting me—A place where none appeared.

Oh, night that guided me, Oh, night more lovely than the dawn,
Oh, night that joined Beloved with lover, Lover transformed in the Beloved!

Upon my flowery breast, Kept wholly for himself alone,
There he stayed sleeping, and I caressed him, And the fanning of the cedars made a breeze.

The breeze blew from the turret As I parted his locks;

With his gentle hand he wounded my neck And caused all senses to be suspended.

I remained, lost in oblivion; My face I reclined on the Beloved.
All ceased and I abandoned myself, Leaving my cares forgotten among the lilies.

—Saint John of the Cross, translation by Edgar Allison Peers[5]

A major blessing at this time was my husband's love and support. Also, I had my horses and my law practice to focus on. Another blessing was that after the rejection from those I had wanted to serve in church and state, I pulled myself back in and spent my time and energy finding healing for myself.

This experience shattered my faith in outer communities, except for my husband. All other pillars of my outer life were erased during this time. This pain, on the heels of experiencing what we humans commonly know as death, but to me was a blissful escape from sometimes cruel life here on Earth, was necessary for my healing journey.

I certainly experienced parts of my being dying daily—and I still do. It seems all those parts of myself, those places where I had defenses and restrictions in my being that blocked me from fully living, had to die for me to move forward and find healing. I began to understand that deep healing is a spherical process. I could almost feel my divine geometry being lit up at different levels. It felt like a grand symphony of music. When one note, or one point of being of my divine geometry, changed—whether for better or worse—that one change modified the entire landscape of my being. So, finding healing in one place of my being would disrupt other parts of my being.

I realized I was not going to feel comfortable because so many parts of me were changing at so many levels. I surrendered to the process and trusted that I would be able to make it to the next resting place on my quest to reach my inner summit of being. Sometimes I preferred focusing on my inner life rather than experiencing my outer life. The healing process taught me that my end goal is integration between my inner and outer worlds as I strive for balance, harmony, and oneness—as above, so below.

As all these things were groaning and travailing inside me, I continued an outer path of healing. I was prompted to seek outside help from my naturopathic doctors, my Chinese medicine practitioner, and from a talented practitioner of somatic bodywork. All these women helped me figure out what was real and what was unreal as I sorted through my habits, defenses, and ways of being that had historically served me but no longer aided me on the path to wholeness. Also, I sought the assistance of several women trained in outer psychology. I ran into Lucile, a counselor, at a spiritual conference, and I asked her if she would help me. She agreed and we commenced therapy.

I confess that part of me has not fully bought into psychological theory. In fact, I am suspicious of and a nonbeliever in almost all theories. I respect those who share their training and hearts to assist others in their healing path. I have been blessed by having had several very skilled professional women, including Lucile, assist me and care for me as I stumbled through my inner wounds to find resolution and peace. I always find that a therapist's ability to love me in an impersonal yet personal way is more conducive to healing than whatever theoretical approach to psychology they adhere to.

During the five years after almost leaving embodiment, Lucile counseled me. I saw one of my two naturopathic doctors at least once per month, did acupuncture, saw a chiropractor, and engaged in daily spiritual practice. Also, I spoke with Dr. Bonnie Greenwell, author of several books on energy transformation and kundalini, because of her unique knowledge around and experience with internal healing changes. At one point, Lucile asked me, in a joking manner, how many mothers I needed. I answered, "I need as many women as the Divine Mother requires to work through to help me heal." I see myself as a devotee of the Divine Mother, and I love any spiritual books that discuss the role of the Divine Feminine. Based on those beliefs and my promise to God to do whatever was necessary to heal, I felt that the Divine Mother would always be with me and provide me with healers.

During those years, I spent tens of thousands of dollars on the services I needed to heal myself in all parts of my being: my spiritual self, my mental self, my emotional self, and my physical body—what are called the four lower bodies. I took herbs and vitamins, did IV therapy, had blood tests, changed my diet, and took a few prescription drugs. Several years into my healing, I went back to see the lung and heart doctors who had kept me alive during the time I was hospitalized. They each did individual imaging tests of my heart and lungs and were almost giddy with relief that neither my heart nor lungs were damaged by the severe inflammation I had suffered. They both told me to keep doing "whatever I was doing," and released me from any follow-up visits with them in their specialties. I believe they thought my recovery was a bit of a miracle.

At one point in the process, I felt guilty about spending so much money and time on this process. I discussed it with my husband. By the end of the conversation, I had decided that even though it might seem prudent to spend money on my retirement plan instead of healthcare, most of which could be categorized as "alternative," the reality was that if I did not heal and live, I would not need any resources for retirement. (Or, maybe one could say I would have retired to another place in God's kingdom instead of residing in a body on Earth.) But much of the healing care that I received was not covered by insurance.

Even though I had received very good care from the hospital in Billings, my experience was that if my insurance would pay for it, the service probably would not heal me, and it might kill me. For example, at one point I was referred to a rheumatologist, who also could not figure out what was wrong with me. I went through a whole battery of tests, and he said I met two-and-a-half of the five requirements for a Lupus diagnosis. Based on that half diagnosis, he wanted me to take a daily prescription requiring blood tests because the medicine could wreck my liver. I realized he wanted to treat me for something I did not really have with a drug that could hurt me, and I decided no, thank you. I do think he was a good doctor, but, if all you have is a hammer, everything looks like a nail. He did not have what I needed to heal. Thank God I said no, because based on what happened after that in my healing path, I believe if I had taken the medicine and stopped my search for a spiritual answer to my health issues, I would not be here writing this book. I believe that if I had followed this doctor's advice I would have died.

Gestalt is a German word that is hard to define in English. In her book *What the Heck Is Gestalt?* Melisa Pearce wrote, "Gestalt leads to wholeness. As a person journeys through their unfinished business, a level of self-awareness allows room for personal responsibility and a life of self-compassion."[6] In 2015, half a year before I wound up in the hospital and left to experience other dimensions and returned to occupy my body, I had an equine Gestalt experience that, though I didn't realize it at the time, prepared me for my healing transformations.

During the summer, I attended an equine Gestalt retreat at my neighbor June's guest ranch called Bonanza Creek. My sister and I were looking for something to do together with horses. Little did we know when we signed up how instrumental this retreat would be for my ability to stay with my body and then pursue wholeness.

At this first retreat led by Jaimie, who had been trained as an Equine Gestalt Coach, I felt seen, heard, and supported by both Jaimie and the horses. This was the first time I really talked about and re-experienced my sexual abuse as a small child. As I shared this trauma, the group of women and horses held me in a sacred place, which helped me to experience the trauma in a loving, supportive atmosphere. This experience opened the door for my healing path.

I had lent June my horse Buddy, who at that time was in his late twenties and was a trustworthy, gentle guest horse for kids or smaller riders. So he lived at Bonanza Creek and while I was there, I got to spend lots of time with him. Having him at the retreat was a huge bonus for me. Tears ran down my cheeks several times during that retreat because I knew Buddy would not be with me much longer. Buddy had already lived beyond the normal lifespan for a horse by that time—late twenties for a horse is like a person being in their eighties.

Buddy helped bring things full circle when he seemed to tell me to open my heart and trust others. I believe he lived longer than most horses to stay with me and help fulfill my reason for being by choosing a path toward wholeness. Buddy also coached other clients that first weekend, and I felt so blessed to have him, my heart horse, there with me.

Buddy's Eye

Buddy's eye is orange-amber with a cobalt-blue center
A unique and strangely colored eye for a horse
Over the years, his eye has changed from wild, rebellious, and self-protecting to soft and languid
It seems I can see God in his eye and it seems God can see me

To see and be seen through Buddy's eye is a slice of heaven on Earth
I wonder . . . does Buddy's eye reflect God's love or amplify God's love?

I have witnessed his transformation from an abused horse to a loving willing partner in our path together

Buddy's internal changes helped fuel my healing transformation

To say Buddy is wise, loving, and powerful is to state the obvious

Buddy's love helped me move forward and open my heart to equine Gestalt coaching, which is when a trained coach partners with a horse that, due to its heightened sensitivity, can be in genuine contact with human emotion. Horses walk away when we are not in a place of authenticity and contact with our hidden emotions. At that first retreat with Jaimie, I started to open my heart and my awareness and discovered that I had less-than-healthy reactions to ongoing events in my world. Buddy's love and support, and a seed of awakening planted at that retreat in the summer of 2015, started to sprout after my experience of being in the light of higher dimensions.

∞

CHAPTER 9

Being Fully Present

After more than fifty years of running from the unbearable pain of my childhood wounds, and after dying and being sent back to finish my reason for being in this body, my first big realization was that I had to slow down so my body and being could rest. Before I left the hospital, and as I was figuring out how to honor my promise to God to seek wholeness, I became aware that my sick body needed sleep to heal. At this time in my life, I had not slept all through the night for decades. Most nights I would have a hard time falling asleep because my unprocessed anxiety increased when I lay down to rest. Something about trusting my body and going into the sleep cycle triggered my PTSD. Also, I hated laying down to sleep and then suffering from my unprocessed emotions and the physical pain still trapped in my body. I had a horrible habit of not sleeping.

To honor God and my promise to do whatever it took to heal, I asked one of my doctors for medication to help me sleep. I knew the medicine was a short-term solution. I also knew that to change my sleep habits, I had to immediately start doing whatever I could to start changing myself so that I could sleep.

In addition to the medication, I started being kind to myself regarding my poor sleep habits and decided to take small steps forward to heal myself at all levels so that I could surrender and sleep without suffering from pain. It was similar to my battle with being overweight—no matter how much I wish I were not fifty pounds overweight, the reality was that I was fifty pounds overweight. No matter how much I wanted to change myself overnight, that was simply wishful thinking and nothing else. To lose weight, I needed to treat myself with kindness and love—not self-criticism and judgment. I needed to eat healthier, eat less, and exercise more. I also needed to start in the reality of where I was, not where I wanted to be. I had to pursue daily practices that would help me gain health, lose weight, and be able to sleep better.

On the practical level, I made sure our bedroom was a safe place that felt good to me. I made sure I did not drink anything with caffeine after noon. I started walking each day to increase my exercise. Also, when I lay down to sleep, I observed myself and tried to gently keep myself from panicking that I would not be able to sleep, as this would cause more pain and lead me to fail. I told myself that this was a never-ending self-story. Instead of doing the same old thing and revolving around that negative story, I substituted prayer. Even though I had been raised Lutheran, I have loved Mother Mary since I was a young child. So I would say to myself over and over when I had trouble falling asleep, "In the immaculate heart of Mary I trust." Gradually, by being kind to myself, exchanging healthy substitutes for my old bad habits, and being consistent in my daily actions, my sleep habits changed.

Now, I am a champion sleeper. I love to go to bed at night and I love to get up in the morning. I usually fall asleep within minutes of going to bed. I still wake up at least once per night, but usually, I realize I am safe and everything is okay. I hear my husband breathing steadily beside me, and I go back to sleep. I am very aware that getting enough sleep is foundational for all aspects of healing. In my case, I did experience miraculous healing, and part of that miracle was repatterning my inner and outer habits to get better sleep.

In addition to that, I also had to develop the inner habit of truly trusting God. Part of the reason I had a hard time sleeping, slowing down, or resting was that I was afraid. At some level, I believed that if I kept moving and never let down my guard, I would be able to keep myself safe. The fear instilled in me from my childhood trauma was subconscious and drove me in ways of which I had no outer awareness.

This unfinished business led me to seek out another therapist. It was a cool, crisp day in September when I first met Heidi Soper in her small studio office located in downtown Bozeman. She was trained in somatic experiencing, which is a practical application of Peter A. Levine's work regarding how the body releases trauma and restores goodness. When I went to see Heidi, I felt overwhelming waves of terror rising inside me. As I felt like I was in danger of becoming unhorsed inside due to those waves, I decided I would handle those parts of myself that felt like bolting similarly to how I handled my horses.

As I have discussed, my lifelong passion for horses began at three or four years old. When I was a child, the place where I experienced oneness with God and started my ongoing conversations with the Divine was when I was alone with my horses. So much of my inner understanding of love and self-mastery comes from what I have learned with horses. Hence, it is a bit automatic for me to look inside myself to review what I have experienced with horses to find ways forward in tough times. I likened my feelings of terror to a fresh young mare that has not yet been handled by people or learned to trust that people will be kind to her. I decided that I would just attempt to hold myself together gently with the reins of self-control, allow my feelings to surface, and see what my time with Heidi would bring. Importantly, due to my experiences with physical trauma, I also told the parts of me that were terrified that we would physically leave if I thought I needed to do that to stay safe.

To keep parts of me from running away, I remembered the oneness I felt from riding one of my horses, Hoss. I recalled the feelings of bliss I experienced when I was so connected with him and how he and I had moved as one being. Buddy had become too old to ride, and I found Hoss. Hoss was the horse I rode during the darkest days of my illness. He was a very tall, dark brown gelding that had been imported from Ireland. Based on his behavior, I thought he had been through some type of trauma. Nevertheless, during some of our rides and time together, Hoss and I connected at a deeper level than I had ever experienced before on any horse.

One day I received a phone call from my barn, and I learned that Hoss had slipped on the ice and broken his pelvis. Since Hoss was more than sixteen hands tall (a hand is four inches), and any horse breaking their pelvis is usually a death sentence, I did not expect him to survive. Still, I called a vet who also did horse chiropractic treatments, and he treated Hoss late on the night of his fall. Fortunately, Hoss's broken pelvis did not rupture an artery, and with the treatment, he survived. We started on a yearlong recovery plan.

As I was slowly working through my own healing, I spent money on and time with Hoss, trying to help him heal. The people who boarded Hoss kept him in their yard for months so he could be separated from other horses and have a safe place to heal. Finally, Hoss was healed enough that I could start leading him out of his pen on walks. Interestingly, his ability to walk coincided with my increased ability to walk and also breathe better. At this point, it seemed that our lives together were looking better.

Then the unthinkable happened. I received another phone call from the boarding barn that Hoss had fallen over backward and was in a lot of pain. I drove out to the barn to see him, and when I went into his stall, Hoss was standing there trembling with his head hanging. I looked him in the eye, and I sensed he was almost out of his mind with pain. My heart told me that I needed to let Hoss go because this time his pain was too much for him to bear. To be sure, I called the vet. She X-rayed him, and we discovered that Hoss had broken bones in his spine around his withers. We decided to put Hoss down because this injury was not one that he could heal from. I felt shocked because it seemed to me that Hoss had purposely caused the injuries that led to his demise, choosing not to live with the pain that was making him crazy.

My driving values of integrity, compassion, and transformational healing had moved me to decide to continue in life and to deal with the pain that had been driving me out of my own mind. I went deep within and decided that my path to wholeness would be to treat my spiritual self, my mental self, my emotional self, and my physical self with love and devotion the same way I would for a horse I loved.

My experience with Hoss pushed me forward in my determination that choosing life was the first critical step to finding a healing path forward.

As I remembered the lessons of Hoss in her office, Heidi explained to me a little bit about what she did. Strangely, even though I had been a journalist and an attorney with good communication skills, I could not hear or understand much of what she said. Suffice it to say that the mere act of asking someone for help and being with her in her office triggered my fight-or-flight response. I was so caught up in the stress response habits of my brain that my neural pathways were overrun, and the other parts of my brain were not online at that time. I could not process her words.

I thought about leaving, and parts of me certainly felt like this healing treatment was a life-or-death experience. These feelings of terror also triggered my brain to create a narrative that I could not trust Heidi. I hardly knew her, so the reality was that I did not yet have enough information to know whether or not I could trust her. But since I had promised God to do whatever it took to become whole, I chose to stay and at least see what she might have to offer to assist my healing journey.

As Heidi touched my feet and legs, I experienced myself grounding in my body a little. However, this was immediately followed by greater terror—I left my body and entered a disassociated state. Apparently, in the fifty or so years of life after my childhood abuse experience, I had created a very effective pain avoidance mechanism of just leaving my body instead of dealing with those deeply stored feelings that I was sure would kill me. She noticed the empty container of my body, so she asked me to gently focus where she was working on my body. She also asked me to open my eyes, look around myself to see that I was safe, and then take my attention inward and focus on what I sensed there. After I focused inward, she asked me to bring my awareness outward again and focus on how the air felt on my skin. She led me in a meditation that helped me to be in my body with awareness and to quiet my inner state of hyperarousal in my amygdala.

Heidi is a very good massage therapist who is also trained in somatic experiencing—a very lovely, kind person. My terror was not caused by her in any way, except that she was the person that I first allowed to touch my body so that I could find a way to access, feel, and release the deep pain that was stored within it. The terror was one hundred percent mine, and her being kind and using her skills to help me heal triggered that terror. To heal, I needed to stop running from and avoiding my inner terror.

Now I know that, based on my healing experience of learning how to stay present and to titrate my terrified feelings when being touched, at some point in my childhood, I decided that anybody getting close enough to touch me could be a hurtful event. Also, I now know that, even though I experienced the pain from abuse from those who were older than me and who were supposed to keep me safe, my childhood experience is no longer an ongoing daily experience in my life. I can choose to leave behind my attachment to and reliving of those memories of trauma and abuse in my body. Until I died and came back, I was still stuck in seeing the world through the cloud of my unresolved trauma. Once I started the healing path, I realized that much of my inner programming that seemed so true is simply no longer real.

For example, part of me thought and felt that Heidi would hurt me if I allowed her to get close to me. That was incorrect, but my instinct to not let anybody near me was probably a good survival strategy when I was a child. However, in her office that day, I no longer needed that ingrained survival strategy.

One of my biggest inner awakenings during my healing path was that no matter how much I tried to modify or retrain my inner reality from projecting out, I could not control it from leaking into my outer life. For example, the part of me that had hardened and decided to never let anyone touch me, or if touched, to be extremely guarded and ready to fight or run, told me strongly not to let Heidi help me. I felt the intense terror and pondered why that part of me reacted so strongly against the process of somatic experiencing. Since I was so strongly driven from the inside to bolt and I did not know whether my feelings were unfounded in this circumstance, I decided to adopt a wait-and-see, observational tactic going forward. I told myself that if I really wanted to leave during a session, I could leave. That gave me the sense that I was safe to move through feeling and then letting go of my deep wounds from the past.

Now that I am on the other side of this healing process, I realize how fractured my view of the world was. It was like I was looking through the kaleidoscope of my wounds. It took time and my new lived experiences of not being hurt for my inner view of my outer world to shift.

One morning during my healing process, I arrived early to our pasture to gather cows. Since I had time on my hands, I decided to soak up the moment with Ruby, my ranch mare. Ruby and I stood on a high hill where we could view the world around us fully. Smells of damp earth, the aftermath of rain, and spring in Montana filled our noses.

Ruby stood there very quietly—unusual for her since she prefers to be on the move, working. But unlike Ruby, my consciousness and being was flitting around on the inside. It was amazing I could even stay in the saddle. I was not present in my body. Then, I decided to pay attention to Ruby. After all, I was sitting on her back. She stood there like a statue, but fully present. I saw her curling her neck from one side to the other, viewing the beautiful panorama. So, I decided to follow her lead and see if I could notice what she was witnessing.

What an experience to meditate high on the hill with Ruby! Together we observed the Canadian geese flying overhead and honking. Then we slowly moved our gaze the other way and just observed clouds moving. We could feel a bit of breeze. It felt like being kissed by nature.

The longer I viewed the world with Ruby, the stiller I became inside and the more present I felt in my body. We had an interval on the hill when we were together in consciousness. I still felt the blessing hours later from taking time to view the world with her. This experience taught me many lessons, some that I am still unpacking. All the major spiritual paths discuss developing an observing mind, a higher consciousness, a Christ mind, or something similar. In the past, I thought I understood this because I read it and thought about it. However, Ruby taught me that until I observed the world around me while being still and fully in my body, I had not experienced it fully.

She taught me that she could see—and also feel—for miles to check for danger. Horses are flight animals and depend on their ability to sense far-off danger and flee for survival. But that day, Ruby did not sense any danger. She was happy to sit up there and just soak in all the life that was happening around her.

After my time on that hill with Ruby (which seemed like the eternal now), I started pondering. What if I observed my life, inner and outer, as I experienced Ruby observing life around us? What if I were able to be serene and present and could trust my senses on how to react to what was happening?

And then, I did start learning to trust my observation and senses. I moved forward and through the somatic experiencing therapy. I was no longer burdened by my inner view skewing everything I experienced. I was able to allow the pain and terror to leave my body, letting go of my strategy of avoidance.

As a child, my number one strategy to avoid feeling pain or terror was to get away from everyone. If I could not physically leave everyone and be alone, I disassociated. By that, I mean that I simply exited my body and allowed myself to exist in a state above and out of my body. I became very masterful at disassociation. I first utilized this means to avoid feeling when I was being sexually abused and have no or very little recollection of experiencing this assault by feeling it in my body.

Instead, I remember looking down upon myself and the neighbor boy.

When I was a little girl riding my Shetland pony and playing with God out in the large pasture on our ranch, I was in my body because I felt safe, and I needed to be present to ride Little Red. He was not very well broke and was a bit ornery, so I learned how to ride Little Red and stay in my body. When I was alone with God and Little Red, I was safe from other people, but I had to be present and aware to be able to manage Little Red so he did not dump me off and hurt me.

As soon as I went back inside the house and became captive to my mom's world, I reverted to disassociating. When I could not be gone physically, I could still be gone in my three other lower bodies; my spiritual, mental, and emotional bodies were absent. This ability to split my lower bodies seemed ingenious when I was a child and allowed me to cope, but it was a huge problem in my adult years.

As I grew up on several different ranches in Montana, there had been times when I was present in my body more fully. To be around horses and to ride for hours straight, one has to be in their body. So, I imagine that horseback riding, which started very early for me, as well as participating in rodeo and three-day eventing all helped me to know how to be present in my body.

Another saving grace was my competitiveness and love of sports. To be good at a physical sport, I had to be in my body. My love of competing in rodeo events and playing basketball and other team sports, such as football, all helped me develop anchoring in my physical body and self-mastery in that quadrant of being. This led to my winning several state titles and playing two varsity sports at the college level. My seven years of working full-time for several months of the year as a horseshoer and blacksmith also helped anchor me in my physical body.

On the other hand, my work as a journalist and an attorney aided my ability to disassociate. In law school, I had to work almost full-time to pay for school, food, housing, and so on. During the day I would attend class, and in the evening I would study, then do research and write for my journalism job. I would often sit and focus on my computer screen or in class for more than sixteen hours per day. I would jokingly say that all my body was used for was to move my head from my pillow to my place of work. I kept up this unhealthy habit for several decades. My ability to focus and concentrate while losing all awareness of my physical surroundings was a boon to my intellectual and writing pursuits, but it led to my many health problems.

After I promised God that I would do whatever it took to heal and get in my body, I often wondered why I made that promise. The promise came from deep within me and seemed to be informed by wisdom that I did not yet understand, including my habit of leaving my body. But once I embarked on my healing path, the promise started to make sense. At first, all I gained was the mere awareness that I felt very resistant to being present in my body and experiencing the emotional and physical pain that I had so adeptly avoided for more than five decades. Before my promise, it would have been my habit to avoid the discomfort that I sometimes felt when I was in my body, but after my promise, I treated myself like a young colt that I was training. When I started to bolt and leave either physically or by disassociating, I would gently pull myself back into my body. I would look around myself to make sure I was safe and then I would use the skills I had learned from Heidi.

If indeed I was in a safe place (which I always was), I told myself, *I am here now.* Then, I would look around me, experience feeling or hearing something on the outer, like the air on my skin or the wind rustling in the trees. Heidi called this "resourcing myself." I learned how to observe when I begin to disassociate and then, instead of allowing that to happen, I would consciously anchor myself in my body.

During my several years of intense healing on the inner and outer, I became aware that I was extremely sensitive, much like a horse. This meant that I could often feel what others around me were feeling.

My first therapist, Dr. Lidren, had described me as being "wired for sound." According to her, it is common for those who have been through trauma as a child or have a parent who is an alcoholic, to be extremely tuned in to the emotional state of others around them as a survival mechanism. As Kelly McDaniel explains in her book *Mother Hunger*, "If you grew up with a mother who was cruel and frightening, her behavior required your autonomic nervous system to stay in overdrive. . . . Like someone anticipating a blow, your body and mind are wired for war."[7] This extreme sensitivity to others and my skill at leaving my body made living in my body very uncomfortable and confusing. I had all my unfinished emotions and physical pain to deal with, and I also felt others' pain and emotions. I did not know where I began and where I ended. I truly only felt safe and comfortable when I was out in nature with my horses or with my dog.

I know it sounds strange, but when I first started my healing path, I lacked the inner mastery to stay united in my body with my four lower bodies. For most of my life, I longed to leave my body and go home to God. Part of me felt that God must have made a mistake and sent me to the wrong place. I didn't like my life on Earth, and my heart's desire then was to move further from my body and move home to oneness with God.

After six years of intense transformational healing at all levels of being, I began to realize that the purpose of my life was to embody my divine identity, my unique geometry of God's light energy. I began to realize that my body was a tremendous blessing, a gift to anchor my real self in a physical being on Earth and embody that light from above. I now know that only with my ongoing embodiment of light will I have the key to my wholeness.

During my time of deep healing, part of me wanted to stay home, both inside myself and literally in my actual home, and not be seen by others. Another part wanted to share, have connection, be seen, and learn how to communicate in ways that inspired others to find their healing path. I decided both parts were right, and the path forward is about coming home to our deep inner connection to source.

I asked myself: *What is source? Why should I be connected to it? How will staying home, being present in my body, enable me to connect to source?* Learning how to stay home was very important to me finding a deep inner connection, inner peace, and harmony. However, it was not just staying home physically, but also metaphorically. In other words, not allowing my attention to escape from my focused awareness in the here and now.

I had to practice maintaining this focus. I had to learn how to listen to someone deeply and hear every word while not thinking about something else or how I might want to respond. Another way I learned to develop my focus was to only think about one thing at a time. Sometimes, my consciousness seemed to chase an emotional squirrel, not a mental one, meaning that a feeling would get triggered. So, instead of staying focused on the here and now, I would get caught up in that feeling. Fear sometimes triggered flashbacks to past trauma. So instead of being here and now where I was safe at home with my husband, in my feeling body, I felt like I was on the verge of personal harm and that nothing could save me.

Instead of bolting in fear, I would gently tell myself, *Whoa,* and bring myself back. I would tell myself, *Let's stop "leaving home" with these emotions and focus on the here and now.* I would tell myself, *I am here now, and I am safe. I can connect with a source of love, and I can receive and share that love.*

I soon discovered that knowing how to stay home with my mind and emotions as well as my physical body was a path toward inner wholeness. Inner wholeness resulted from me developing an inner sense of well-being that began to permeate my outer consciousness. Staying home in my four lower bodies was key to my consciousness being filled with goodness, love, and a desire to fulfill my reason for being. I discovered and made friends with parts of myself that I came to like.

Once I became more adept at staying home, I realized that, just like a bucket with a hole that leaks water, I had a wound in my heart, a hole in my being that could not be filled. The unconscious actions of my mom and the sexual abuse by the neighbor boy broke my heart to create the hole in my being. My vessel was leaky. So, no matter what, neither God, my husband, nor anyone else could fill me up.

The love of my horses and doing my inner work to heal through Gestalt gradually allowed my heart to heal. My ability to stay home in my lower bodies and live wholeheartedly kept expanding moment by moment, day by day, as I spent time with my horses in nature and was able to be more and more present. As I lived with more love for all of life around me, including people, my horses and dogs responded to me differently than what I experienced before my inner healing.

∞

CHAPTER 10

Compassion Is Key

∞

My cow dog Rosie has been the latest addition to my life. She has no fear of me and has helped me become aware of how bad I was at truly trusting God. My sister raised her and then brought her to my husband and me when she was nine weeks old. We met in the middle, several hundred miles from each of our ranches, so we could pick her up. I asked my husband to drive home because I wanted to hold Rosie on my lap so she would bond with me. My strategy worked, and we have spent the last few years learning from each other.

I have never hit her or hollered at her in anger. We all know we are not supposed to do those things, but with my prior dogs, I had always failed at least once or twice. I sometimes failed at managing my emotions. I wanted to keep my dogs safe and felt scared or got mad when they did not behave or listen to me. At any rate, even though I cannot remember the exact circumstances, I am pretty sure that until Rosie, I was not able to control myself to not get after my pet in anger at times.

I learned that attempting to manage my emotions is a step on the path to wholeness. I also now know that, until I allowed my inner life to be transformed by God's transformational love and support, I really could not completely control my reactions and subsequent actions. Everything I experienced in life filtered through the perspective created by restrictions and the unreal self I created to protect myself. Apparently, at a deep level, I did not trust God to protect me. At a deep level, I felt unworthy of God's love and protection.

Since I have never hit Rosie, she only expects love and support from my hands. When I pick her up, she often exposes her belly in her surrender to total comfort in my lap. She seems to know no worry about her safety or whether she is loved. She looks me in the eye with total connection and belief that she is worthy of love. Rosie adores me. She trusts me. She (mostly) listens to me.

There are several things I have realized from these past few years with Rosie. First, I have not continued forward my mom's behavior of sometimes punishing those who depended on her. Second, I am not as trusting or lovingly obedient in my relationship with God as Rosie is in her relationship with me. Even though God has never hurt me, underneath I still fear that he might. Even though I have been on a spiritual path and growing a daily spiritual practice, I still harbor this inner mistrust because of my unfinished business of resolving my childhood traumas.

Although I was given the miracle of life and stayed with my body here on Earth, I still had to face and conquer those places in me that were not in congruence with my true self. These were horrible feelings and places inside me that I had spent nearly fifty years trying to avoid at all costs. Even though I lived through it, I often wonder how I summoned enough courage to continue forward on this path into feeling that which I thought would kill me. Why would anyone choose to feel so uncomfortable?

Did you ever wonder why somebody would choose to climb Mount Everest or one of the other highest peaks in the world? For those of us who are not mountain climbers, it is hard to fathom why one would train for months, strap on oxygen, and venture out into the elements to climb to the top of a barren rock in an adventure that could result in the loss of their outer life. While most of us do not have that urge, maybe there is a similar drive that pushes some of us to climb what seems like an inner mountain to find health and wholeness.

In addition to wanting to accomplish my reason for being, I also knew that having a body within which to uncover the mysteries of healing and wholeness was a gift that I did not want to waste. I now believe having a body provides a container and crucible for honesty, which I believe is important for anyone to awaken to their true nature and divine identity.

I have always believed in God and that there is much to life that is not easily apparent to my outer eyes. My parents believed in a higher power and my two brothers, my sister, and I were brought up attending Sunday school in the local Catholic church, in addition to family services in the Lutheran church. My way of talking to God was my own, supplemented by the church services we sometimes attended. When things were rough at home, I went out to the great outdoors and escaped to spend hours alone with my horses. This is when I felt safe and talked to God.

Since my structured religious education was secondary to my inner, ongoing relationship with God, when I attended church, I started to understand what many others thought about the spiritual path. Yet I had my own inner direction and did not really care if my direction coincided with others' beliefs. I had always known that each of us was created uniquely by the Divine and that just like no two snowflakes were alike, each of us has our own divine geometry. My religious studies also led me to the Climb the Highest Mountain series by Mark Prophet and Elizabeth Clare Prophet. When I found these books, I realized that, just like some people were compelled to climb outer mountain peaks, I had a passion to climb the highest mountain peak of all, to oneness with God.

In walking the path to wholeness, I have come to believe that I forgot my divine identity by covering it up with a maze of defenses, wounds, avoidant behaviors, and other mechanisms as a way to keep myself from feeling hurt, pain, unsafe, and all those feelings I wanted to avoid. So as I continued moving forward with the courage to pursue healing and wholeness, I began to understand that my reward for going through the labyrinth of my unreal identity creation—in other words, my psychology—was that I sometimes began to find myself in a state of great peace, feeling deep love, or just simply feeling free to exist as I truly am.

American clinical psychologist, psychotherapist, teacher, and author John Welwood is known for integrating psychological and spiritual concepts, and I find his writing and teaching to be the gold standard for the healing journey of the heart to embody wholeness. In his book *Toward a Psychology of Awakening* he wrote, "If we try to avoid the rawness and tenderness of the heart, we will become trapped in our character armor, which we initially developed to protect our vulnerable feeling centers."[8] Further, he explained, "To be fully human is to forge bridges between earth and sky, form and emptiness, matter and spirit. And our humanness expresses itself in a depth and tenderness of feeling or *heart* that arises at the intersection of these poles."[9]

Another author, teacher, and psychologist, Jack Kornfield, wrote, "The wisdom of the heart is here, just now, at any moment. It has always been here, and it is never too late to find it. The wholeness and freedom we seek is our true nature, who we really are."[10] It seems one of the great mysteries of all the world's religions is that our ability to connect to divine consciousness is here and now, yet most of us just ignore the opportunity. So, a true reason to walk into our wounds and assess our real self through the portal of pain and discomfort is to find the wisdom and wholeness of the heart, which opens doors to the higher consciousness that is available to us.

When I first started to be responsible for my health on all levels of my being, I pondered where to start. I realized that I needed to take the first step from where I was at the moment. This lesson was driven home for me one day when there was an opening between early winter storms at our ranch. I decided I had better pull the horses' shoes and trim our two ranch horses before the next snowstorm and brutal temperatures hit. I walked to the pasture to get the horses, caught them, walked them into the barn, and an hour after starting, I was finally ready to work on the task of removing their shoes and then trimming their feet.

Now, in case you do not know, anything to do with horse hooves is just plain hard work. More than thirty years ago, I sometimes shod or trimmed seven to ten horses per day. Now, however, I mostly work as an attorney at a desk writing on my computer and talking on the phone. Suffice it to say, I am older and not in the physical shape I once was when I made my living shoeing horses.

After getting the horses off their hill and down to our ranch buildings, I had to round up my tools, since I do not use them that often anymore. Of course, I forgot a necessary tool and had to walk back and forth between ranch buildings gathering all that I needed. By the time I started pulling shoes, I had been out walking for an hour and a half. I started to get worried about whether I would have the energy to pull the shoes and trim eight hooves after the physical exertion I had already done.

I kept telling myself, *Just keep moving forward. You can rest if you need to.* Soon, after working on a few feet and moaning and groaning while pulling the shoes off, I had shed all my warm clothing and was standing there in my t-shirt, dripping sweat. My inner voice was telling me, *I do not like this.* But I just kept putting one foot in front of the other and focused on helping my horses. If I did not accomplish the task, the horse's feet would ball up with snow and ice, which makes it very hard for them to walk up and down the hills. I did not want them to slip around and potentially get hurt in the next storm, so I kept working and removing the shoes.

As I was working on this task, dripping sweat, and pondering how much I did not like the present moment, I realized how much of life that is worth attaining creates moments like this, when hard work causes me to feel discomfort. I could just quit and leave the horses half-done or even with too-long hooves and shoes, which might cause them to slip and hurt themselves. Or I could focus on the task at hand, keep on moving toward the goal one step at a time, and be done.

I did finish pulling shoes and trimming the horses' hooves. In retrospect, my dislike or discomfort with the job seemed very minor compared to what it felt like when I was dripping sweat, wondering whether I had the outer or inner resources to finish the task. I am grateful that I was able to keep on keeping on. I am grateful I cared enough that I could push myself past what seemed like my limit.

Similarly, I have experienced that moving into and through inner transformation has times when it seems like I cannot or do not want to move through resistance. Yet, I have found that the best place to start is where I am. Then I take the first step and just keep moving forward until I am done. In the same way, my inner work to find greater peace, harmony, and compassion was not nearly as ominous as it seemed before starting or at some points during the process.

One thing that my horse Buddy taught me was compassion. Since he had been abused and did not trust me when he arrived at my home when he was fourteen, to develop a trusting relationship with him, I had to show him that I was trustworthy and that I would be kind to him. He also expected me to be fair.

Another well-known author, Kristin Neff, wrote, "Compassion literally means to suffer with,"[11] or, in other words, being a friend and companion to the pain that's involved in being human. Buddy had experienced the pain of being a horse in the world of a human who beat him. To gain Buddy's trust, I had to be patient with him when he jumped back in fear of being physically struck. I had to be kind and show him that not all people would hurt him. Buddy, like many horses, has a good heart. He wanted to believe that I could be kind. I just had to prove my ability to consistently treat him with kindness to gain his trust.

In the healing process, I experienced the same thing from the parts of my own soul that had fragmented due to my psychological wounds. To heal and bring those parts home to live in wholeness, I needed to be patient and kind and show those parts that I was trustworthy. I needed to allow the fires of compassion to burn in my heart to create a magnet for the fragmented parts to find their way home to me.

There are many understandings of what compassion is. Nisargadatta Maharaj, a spiritual teacher of nonduality, said, "The consciousness in you and the consciousness in me, apparently two, really one, seek unity and this is love."[12] When Buddy and I began to trust each other and found unity, we found love. My love helped him heal and his love helped me heal.

Buddy's Shedding

It is Spring and Buddy is shedding his heavy winter coat
The dreadlocks of unneeded protection are falling away
His smooth, beautiful coat of many colors is shining through
He sheds the dead coat with ease and never exerts effort to get the itchy, unnecessary covering off him
Buddy does not need his coat for the next season of his life
Maybe it is similar for us when we shed portions of ourselves that are no longer needed
What if we easily shed the dreadlocks of those parts of us that used to protect us from outside storms
What if we allowed our beings to easily release those unnecessary parts of us
What if we exerted little effort to help release the coating that kept us from shining through with inner brilliance
Maybe inner transformation could be as simple as Buddy shedding his winter coat

∞

CHAPTER 11

Integration and Embodiment on the Path

∞

During my healing process, I went through a rough time when I was in the middle stage of resolving, letting go, and realizing that my true self was not my set of defenses. Over the years, I had created these habits in feelings, thinking, consciousness, and unconsciousness, but these habits were not my real God identity. John Welwood wrote that "a complete path of inner development that addresses both our personal psychology and our deeper spiritual nature must involve all three principles—grounding, letting go, and awakening the heart."[13] At the time I was descending into my core wounds, I had not read Welwood's book, but I can see now that my process did involve grounding, letting go, and awakening my heart.

Welwood described a disconnection from our being as a result of the wounds from our "childhood as we contracted in fearful reaction to an environment that did not fully see, welcome, or accept us."[14] Similarly, Melisa Pearce likens the core wound to being struck by lightning. This is when we made choices about how we had to protect ourselves from the world around us. These choices often became the planks of our inner architecture that we laid to establish defenses so we would not feel the fear, pain, discomfort, and other negative things that most souls feel as a result of being embodied.

Similarly, another author, Judith Blackstone, wrote in her book, *The Enlightenment Process*:

> Some of the patterns in our field of being are simply lines of movement, well-traveled paths of response to painful circumstances that happened repeatedly in childhood and that are "triggered" by similar situations in the present. If these patterns are repeated often enough they begin to rigidify in the physical body. The physical tissues of the body harden along the lines of the repeated pattern. These patterns, as I have said, preserve the memory, the mentality of our age, and the emotion of our bound response to the painful circumstances. They also preserve the movement of our organism into the bound position. These patterns also rigidify in our body if they occur when we are very young (the younger we are, the more impressionable) or if our emotional response to a situation is extremely painful (if the trauma is severe). [15]

At the age of four or five, as a result of the double trauma of my mom choking me and the sexual abuse from the teenage neighbor boy, I decided to be tough no matter what and take care of myself. I do not remember making this decision; however, I remember this being my underlying defense mechanism throughout much of my life.

When I first worked with Heidi, I took my clothes off and got under the sheets for the massage. Talk about feeling vulnerable—I was mostly naked. As I recall, my body was pretty jumpy, and I had a hard time staying in my body and present as she gently touched me. When I would escape into another realm and start pondering the beautiful colors I was seeing and experiencing, she would gently ask me to return to the present. She asked me to open my eyes and to see that I was safe. Upon returning to my body, I felt frightened, I could sense my breath being high in my chest, and I felt nausea in my stomach. When I focused and experienced being in the room, in my body, I was able to settle into starting to feel like I was safe.

To me, it seemed like working with Heidi to slowly repattern my habits of escaping my body was kind of like training a puppy. We went slow. We reinforced my efforts to stay present, and she gently pulled me back when I disassociated. I did not like my body. I did not want a body. I wanted to be one with God's consciousness and still felt a little frustrated with God for sending me here.

As we slowly, gently retrained my nervous system and me to be able to reexperience the undealt-with trauma still buried in my emotional and physical bodies, I gradually became more adept at coming home to myself. I learned to like being in my body more than escaping to more amorphous realms of consciousness. Also, the more embodied I became, the better I became at working with my horses.

At this time, I was taking lessons for dressage and found that being more anchored in my body assisted me at multiple levels with riding. I previously mentioned my dressage horse, Hoss, who was highly trained to jump, and we progressed rapidly together. At times while riding

Hoss, I would feel that all time and space had stopped. All I experienced was this divine connection and oneness with Hoss. In those moments, he and I moved as one. My thoughts were his thoughts. His movements were my movements. I felt the divine oneness that I sometimes felt when listening to very good classical music or experiencing the profound beauty of a sunrise. This feeling of connection and oneness stayed with me through my deep healing processes.

I experienced times of extreme connection that elevated me to a flow state and greater spiritual connection, and then I would remember to focus on that feeling when I went back for more bodywork. I was starting to learn new ways of self-mastery that helped me move forward on the path of healing. One of those new ways was focusing on a favorable flow state of consciousness, which, when I remembered to do so, I could then feel in my body. Whenever I started to experience the symptoms of PTSD, I would practice holding both the state of feeling PTSD and the state of feeling safe and at peace in my awareness simultaneously. When I became more adept at holding these two diametrically opposed consciousnesses in my awareness at the same time, I actually began to notice a shift in which I experienced the feelings of fear, terror, shallow breathing, and nausea less and less. I believe this is what author Michael Singer was talking about when he wrote that the transmutation of energy "involves using the rising energy as a positive force by allowing it to cleanse whatever was blocking it."[16]

At one of my weekly appointments, I told Heidi that I did not feel good, so maybe bodywork was not what I needed. She wisely suggested that we should just do a light session and she would work on my hands. I wanted to run from her office. I was terrified of her working on my hands and me sitting next to her where she could see me. I was starting to experience the fear of being seen and heard that was at my core. I felt raw, visceral terror. But I had promised God that I would do whatever it took to become whole, and so far, Heidi had done nothing to harm me. Dr. Lidren also thought the process was good for me and had said if I did not like something, I could leave at any time. So, between the awareness of my promise to God and my awareness that I did not have to stay and do anything I did not want to, I was able to sit on the couch and allow her to massage my hands.

My hands had also been a source of much pain in my life. Working as a blacksmith and horseshoer in my twenties meant a lot of pounding with a hammer and using other hand tools. When I had fibromyalgia, my hands often hurt the worst of any place on my body. Also, the records that were stuck in my body from the childhood trauma were connected to feelings of heartbreaking deep sadness and disappointment in not being cared for and kept safe by my caretakers. So, looking back, I now know that the energy in my hands was very blocked and that one way to help my heart heal was for this energy to be released.

In hindsight, I realize that this may have been one of the biggest breakthroughs on my healing path. I finally trusted myself enough to be seen, to sit close to another human being, and to wait to experience if they would help or hurt me. By this time, I had learned enough inner mastery to tolerate and explore physical and emotional feelings. I had learned to observe and be curious about my feelings and know that my feelings were like the weather—they would often change—and sometimes were not even real. I am not saying that I did not feel what I felt. What I am saying is that I was learning that my feelings were memories from the past and that these feelings were not tied to my current reality, except by memory of the past.

Heidi also did the Arvigo Techniques of Maya Abdominal Therapy, which I experienced as her rubbing my belly in a circular direction. This seemed like she was rubbing Aladdin's lamp, and the treatment did not trigger any reactions at the time. My research on the therapy indicates that it is meant to restore blood flow, support the lymph and nervous systems, and use chi energy to correct the positions of the uterus and other organs.[17] Soon after the treatment, I felt energy start to flow in my solar plexus and seat of the soul area, which is right below the belly button. At first, it was a trickle of energy. However, just a trickle of water can wear down a mountain, and that trickle of energy started working through multiple places in my body that were stuck and stagnant.

The energy centers at the navel and just below are incredibly important places in our body to anchor the light of God. As I heard Mother explain once, when we are seated and naturally place our hands in our lap, it is like forming a cradle for our soul—that is the seat of the soul energy center. I certainly felt like my healing path was bringing my soul home into integration with my divine identity within the container of my physical body.

I began to make inner shifts in awareness and self-mastery that seemed to match the energy flow that was starting to move in my body. And at some point, I finally relaxed more into the process of working with Heidi. I do not remember the date, but I vividly recall lying on the massage table and feeling great light fill my body. During the massage, Heidi made sweet, cooing noise like a mother would for her baby. I was almost overwhelmed by the feeling of light, the expansion of my consciousness, and the triggering of those places that were still stamped with trauma signatures. She commented that she felt something shift, like my soul came into my body or that I was reborn. I said I felt the same way. This event marked another shift in my healing path, and now that this energy was present and flowing, it led to the rest of the healing journey. I did my best to stay in the flow. Since I had some mastery in riding and training young horses, I decided to treat myself and this new energy flowing through me similarly to riding a colt. I tried not to react, to sit relaxed so as to not trigger the colt's anxiety, and to be softly focused and alert so I could roll with whatever the colt might do.

Bonnie Greenwell wrote the book *Energies of Transformation*, and in it, she discussed the cross-cultural concept that spiritual awakening occurs when people connect with energy and light, and experience elevation of their consciousness when people embody the energies of transformation.[18] She discussed Taoism and the practice to stimulate the circulation of chi, or energy and light, through the body. In her explanation, Greenwell quoted from the ancient text *T'ai Chin Hua Tsung Chi*, which was translated by Richard Wilhelm in *The Secret of the Golden Flower*:

> Connection with the primal spirit of the inner Self allows one to "overcome the polar opposites of light and darkness and tarry no longer in the three worlds (earth, heaven and hell)." In Taoist practices, in order to experience "primal spirit" one must subjugate ordinary consciousness or ego through the circulation of light. Through this practice the spirit comes alive, to dominate the heart, and the breath begins a continual circulation.
>
> Then the spirit must be allowed to dive down into the abdomen (solar plexus). The energy then has intercourse with spirit, and spirit unites with the energy and crystallizes itself. This is the method of starting the work. In time the primal spirit transforms itself in the swelling of life into the true energy.[19]

One night after the energy flowed into my body at multiple levels, I woke up from a dream that seemed more real and vivid than my outer life. During this dream, I felt nauseous and had pain in my pelvic area. Also, I felt fear, as if I were on the edge of an abyss of deep despair, sadness, and grief. I wanted to leave my body, but I remembered the self-mastery I had been learning from Heidi. I decided to apply what I had been learning. I tried to focus on my breath and observe my feelings. I cried a little.

In this dream experience, I became aware that I could see myself in the rubble of the Twin Towers on 9/11. Everything had collapsed around me, and I was stuck in the rubble. I was not safe because no structures remained. I could not crawl to safety because the sharp rubble was unstable and would cut or collapse around me and kill me if I moved. I could not crawl to where I used to be because that structure had collapsed in a heap and no longer existed. I was frozen in place. I did not know if there was more danger to come. I did not know if help would arrive. I decided to focus on my breath and to see if I could ride the experience out. I felt sick to my stomach, like I was going to puke. I attempted to pray, breathe, and stay in my body.

During the terror of this experience, I seemed to forget about how to pray, except I remembered Kuan Yin mantras and I asked for the Goddess of Mercy to help me. During my time with the church, I often prayed the rosary to Mother Mary, and along with reciting Christian prayers also learned mantras to Kuan Yin. I settled into a seemingly safe spot in the rubble of disaster around me. The collapsed buildings and heaps of downed structures around me seemed to stop swaying. I felt like I had created a tiny island where I attempted to start feeling safe with Kuan Yin and staying with my body. My feelings of nausea got better, but my head started hurting. In my in-between consciousness, I was also aware that my dog crawled under the covers to snuggle with me. My cat lay on my feet.

I remember thinking, *Maybe this too shall pass, and I will not lose a whole night of sleep.* The pelvic pain increased, and when it reached a certain place, I also felt a great fear of my past deep illness being triggered again. I feared that the extreme inflammation would return and that I would not be able to function. I feared losing my business, not being able to pay my debts, or that I might die.

Again, I brought my awareness to my breath. I felt the tangible softness of my dog against my legs. I kept bringing my attention to my tactile senses. But my body seemed to repel my focused awareness by revealing deeper pelvic pain. I felt there was no place for me to rest and find refuge. Slowly the intensity lifted, and I was able to follow my prayers and focus on my breath to move into a more peaceful, harmonious state of consciousness. I did go back to sleep and lost any remaining awareness of this dream that had seemed more real than life itself.

Soon after this experience, I felt vulnerable and extremely raw, as if my protective armor no longer existed around me. I felt like a walking wound, with no protective barrier between me and the world outside me. It was like the scabs had been removed from my wounds. I felt soft, sore, exposed, and out in the open with nowhere to hide from the outer world that had caused me so much pain.

Even though I felt out of sorts, I still had a six-figure law practice to run and four employees who relied on me for their jobs. Also, I had numerous clients with complex legal problems they paid my office to advise them on. Each morning, I woke up without my typical armor and the gusto it provided, and I wondered how I would be able to practice law when I felt so raw and exposed. I prayed and asked for the intercession of angels to help me and those I served each day.

Looking back upon my experience, I realize that my more than twenty-year habit of going to my office, putting all of myself aside, and focusing totally on serving my clients was a saving grace. Before I reached my office, it seemed impossible that I would be able to concentrate and work. Once I sat at my desk and fell into my habit of total focus on fulfilling my legal profession, I no longer experienced the lack of armor. Once I focused and engaged with all my heart and being, I had better focus and increased ability to serve my clients than I had before my deep healing experiences.

When I would go home after work, all those parts of me that I had tried to ignore and avoid would start surfacing. Again, I felt extremely raw and uncomfortable—like I wanted to bolt. However, where would I run to? Wherever I went there I was. I suppose I could have tried to work 24/7 so I could focus on serving others and never feel those parts of myself that were no longer frozen in the armor of my unreal self.

During this part of my path, I would awaken sometime between 1:00 and 3:00 a.m. and not be able to go back to sleep. I felt so full of love for God and all life, I would have to get up and pray, do the rosary, sing bhajans (Indian devotional chants), or in some way voice and channel the deep love and light flowing throughout my being and body. I worried about my strange behavior because I felt such a duty to my clients, and I thought I would not be able to serve them without adequate sleep. I mentioned my early arising for prayer to Heidi, and she said that the behavior probably would not last. She was correct. I only had a few months of waking up early in the morning, feeling a sense of great expansion and love of the Divine that had to be expressed as it flowed through my body.

At that time in my life, I had been engaged in a daily spiritual path for thirty years that included one-half to two hours per day of devotional prayers, decreeing (some call this chanting), or singing. I had studied the mystical teachings of most of the world's religions and was seeking a path of walking in Jesus Christ's footsteps to embody oneness or union with the light of God. My devotional practice provided me with a specific framework and understanding to help me integrate the love and light flowing into me. However, the process did scare me at times, and I felt like I was out of control and might lose my mind. In some ways, I did lose my mind. Or, in other words, I lost the mind of me that held together all my defenses and restrictions against flowing with a higher consciousness. Yet, this process of falling apart to find wholeness was hard, scary, and all-consuming on multiple levels of being.

Based on multiple teachings I had studied, I understood that it was my outer identity, which some might call the ego or synthetic image, that reinforced the illusion that I was separate from God's being. Some would call my state of consciousness at that time a false belief in duality. The spiritual light that had started flowing in my body created the beginning of new awareness for me. Bonnie Greenwell, who wrote her first book in the 1990s for people in the West who were going through the transformational process and coping with what happens in one's body and being when spiritual energy started flowing, wrote:

> This book is about the subtle energy of the life force, the pure consciousness beyond mind and the ecstatic experience of spiritual awakening. It also tells

of physical collapse, psychic chaos, and personality upheaval, those elements of human transformation that uproot individuals to the core.[20]

For many months between the hours of 8:00 a.m. and 5:00 p.m. on the days I was working, I experienced what seemed like hell through personality upheaval and psychic chaos as I was uprooted from the core of my being. This experience helped me understand why some people might drink to try to numb or avoid feelings that arise inside during transformation. I, too, at one time had used alcohol to try to numb my movement into uncomfortable feelings. Since I promised God that I would do whatever it took to become whole, I realized I could no longer drink or use other means to avoid my inner changes. So I did my best to ride the bucking broncos of my inner feelings and concepts of self as they came unwound.

My several-decade habit of practicing law, and the groove in my being that the habit created, allowed me to make my way back to my left brain and practice law and serve others. During this time, I was lead counsel in several trials, and I prevailed in those cases. Still, once I stepped away from my heavily structured left-brained existence, I felt like I was falling apart. Now, part of me liked what felt like a freer existence when I swung into the right hemisphere of my brain when I was not working. Other parts did not like the strangeness of how it felt. I did not like how I felt when my identity was so amorphous; I did not know who I really was.

It was during these times after work that I felt so naked, I had no outer personality structure to hold me together. During these times of great expansion was also when the parts of myself, which I had denied and kept relegated to deep, dark places inside me, came out to express their unhappiness and judgment. My inner and outer training had prepared me to know that I should not react to or engage in dialogue with this critical, judgmental voice, yet it was hard to avoid because these words were coming from inside me. In my spiritual belief, all of us were created by God in his image, and the purpose of life on Earth is to follow Jesus in uniting with our divine geometry or our unique identity in God. So, not knowing what else to do, I would use my powers of concentration to focus on a mystical depiction of my God-self.[21]

I told myself that I was nothing except my oneness with God—all else was an illusion. I told myself I believed in God, that he created me, just like he created all life. To help me make it through the tough times when I felt like I had no outer identity, I also told myself that any true practice resulted in physical results. Based on my spiritual studies, I understood that at some point on the spiritual path, whatever I had created without God in my consciousness would collapse and that the embodied light would re-create my divine identity in place of that which would not withstand the fire and light of God. I tried to find comfort in my belief that I was experiencing a transformative healing process, even though I felt naked, exposed, out of control, and lost at many levels.

Even though my spiritual studies helped me in many ways, I also suffered from using my spiritual awareness to try to avoid the feelings of hell that seem to arise during transformational healing. John Welwood explained in his book what he perceived as a tendency in members of many spiritual communities. He called this tendency "spiritual bypassing."[22] He wrote, "I noticed a widespread tendency to use spiritual practice to bypass or avoid dealing with certain personal or emotional 'unfinished business.'"[23] Like many of the members of spiritual communities that Welwood had encountered, I had cultivated my spiritual practices and understanding as a means to bypass the hard, painful, sometimes scary work of surrendering the old me to be remade by the light. This revelation reminds me of Jesus's teaching that God cannot pour new wine into old skins. I believe this teaching is directly on point regarding the hard inner work that comes along with transformational healing. Also, I realized I was arrogant, and that thirty years of spiritual study had created a means for me to try and avoid this messy, hard work of sorting through and resolving my stuff, my inner unreality.

My lifelong habit of using disassociation as a means to avoid feeling pain, combined with my awareness of spiritual teachings, allowed me to use my spiritual path as a means to avoid doing my soul work and feeling the pain of life. In my studies of the saints, I read about their suggestions that the portal to oneness with God was to surrender to the pain and suffering that we all experience on some level as a result of being embodied here on Earth. However, I did not expect or want to feel pain or suffering in my body or emotional being. Finally, I surrendered and trusted that God was in charge and I was in the right place.

During this intense process of my inner core unwinding from those restrictions and defenses that I had adopted to protect myself, I began to fully understand the spiritual teaching of "with all thy wanting, want God." Desire is a very strong-willed part of our beings.

It was also at this time that I started to relate to the different parts of myself as horses. I saw my spiritual body as a white stallion that did not cause trouble in my world. However, my mental body, which I saw as a bay stallion, often went charging around causing wrecks for the wagon of my being. My emotional body was a palomino mare, and she was pouty, opinionated, and oftentimes just wanted her way no matter what. Lastly, I saw my physical body as a larger brown, draft cross mare. She paid the price when my emotional and mental body horses ran off in different directions, crashing my whole system. At that time, the four horses were not working as a team. But my draft cross mare put her hoof down and said she would not move forward until all four horses worked together in harmony.

∞

CHAPTER 12

Healing My Heart with Horses

∞

Finally on my way to yes
I hear
I listen
I no longer run
I feel, I acknowledge, I accept the pain
The pain is ancient, dusty, crusty, rusty
Like barnacles clinging to the underside of a submerged vessel
I touch the pain, it allows me in
I groan, I writhe, I moan, I cry
The pain finally has a voice
The pain talks to my heart
My heart talks to the pain
They talk, they connect, they share, they weep
I surrender to the connection
Through the eye of the needle, I burst
I merge with pain
I fuse with love
I feel whole
I feel Holy
I am grateful

It is a Jungian concept that wholeness is a state in which the consciousness and the unconscious work together in harmony. The statement "until you make the unconscious conscious, it will direct your life and you will call it fate," is also commonly attributed to Carl Jung. After three years into my multiyear deep healing journey, I experienced the freeing of many of my repressed thoughts and feelings. I was starting to feel healthier at multiple levels. I decided that I wanted to help others find their wholeness, so I signed up for one of Melisa Pearce's two-year courses on the Equine Gestalt Coaching Method. At the time I began the program, I needed an outer place, a community and a teacher who would help me navigate the release of all the feelings and ideas I had stuffed down in my subconscious. I took the course to heal myself; I did not know that I would love coaching others and that this would become part of my reason for being.

As part of our coursework in the program, each student had to attend eight different four-day weekend courses. Since we were learning how to partner with horses to coach others to find their inner path to wholeness, we would meet in an indoor arena. At one of the schooling sessions, Melisa was talking to one of her horses. This horse had not partnered with a person in the coaching process yet. Melisa told the horse, "You cannot get this wrong." She asked the horse to be present and have confidence and do what came naturally. I decided at that time that I, too, couldn't get it wrong, if I stayed present, centered, and acted with compassion for whomever I was coaching. I also decided that self-compassion was key to my forging ahead on my healing path.

In her class, Melisa taught that in Gestalt, this is called perturbation—experiencing old trauma in a new way that resolves the trauma once and for all. Perturbation is similar to when a liquid reaches a boiling point, and the vapor pressure of the liquid is equal to the pressure exerted on the liquid by the surrounding atmosphere.

My feelings of physical and emotional discomfort built up for several days before the training began. I arrived late because, in my state of emotional arousal, I was not very good at reading the directions or following them. I got lost and arrived in a panic. On the first evening of the session, the twelve women in the training checked in with Melisa and each other and went over what we were going to learn and experience over the next three days. The next morning, I arrived at the barn, feeling physically sick to my stomach and desiring to end my total emotional and physical discomfort. I wanted to bolt away from the arena and my teacher, but I held myself from leaving. In my experience, feeling the pressure build at all levels of being and maintaining my forward climb through my unhealed stuff would lead to a transformative or healing experience.

As part of our learning, we each had the opportunity to work on personal stuff that was holding us back from being fully present. Melisa called on several other women in attendance ahead of me, and by lunchtime, I was so sick to my stomach with anticipation, I did not even eat. I was sure I would throw it all up. Finally, after lunch, she asked me if I would like to do a piece of work with her. Inside, a part of me said, *No way. I am leaving.* Another part said, *This is why I drove for five hundred miles.* I joined her at the front of the group.

There were parts of me that did not want to step up to join her in front of the round corral where Eddie, a beautiful gray Quarter Horse, was doing his first coaching. I had been drawn to Eddie when I first arrived at the barn. My heart led me to him, and he came up to me, nuzzled my face gently, and proceeded to lick my hands. Later I learned that horses lick people's hands when their hearts are blocked because a natural flow of love goes through our hands. Eddie sensed that my heart was blocked, and he used his muzzle and tongue to encourage my heart to open through my hands.

Now I was joining Eddie and Melisa in front of the group. There were eleven students there including me. I moved through the chairs to the front, and Melisa asked me a few questions. I shared with her that I felt nauseous. She was able to ascertain that the source of my emotionally and physically stuck feelings was from my early childhood.

Usually, when we are in training, we put microphone headsets on so everyone at the training can hear and learn from the process. This time Melisa said that I would not need the microphone because my work was going to be about pre-verbal trauma. She asked several of the attendees to get a horse blanket and spread it on the ground. I looked at her and told her, "Oh no, I am not laying on that blanket." At that time, part of me was very conscious of the group of women watching me. I felt self-conscious, and I certainly did not want them to see me fall apart. I did not know them, and I did not trust them. But Melisa said, "Trust me, Hertha." We had done several sessions of private work on my trauma prior to this. I pondered her request, and I decided that, based on my experience with her and her trained coaches, I could trust her. Now was the time to see if I could let go of some of the pain, agony, and other burdens I had been carrying inside all my life.

She told me she heard keening bottled up inside me. I did not answer her. I was strongly resisting feeling what she seemed to want me to explore and experience. I followed her direction and lay down on the blanket. Melisa asked me to curl up like I might envision my little niece or nephew when they were taking a nap. As soon as I moved to lie on my side and brought my knees up a little bit, my body automatically seemed to find comfort in the fetal position. Deep inside I felt a crackling of feelings, and I feared that allowing these feelings to surface might kill me. The feelings were so big and so old and so stuck, I had never felt safe exploring them. Melisa told me I could cry or make a noise if it felt like it might help me move through where I was. I felt so scared to surrender to feeling this deep sadness that was painful and all-encompassing.

Not only had I never cried in front of people before, but I also had never cried the many tears I had stored up from my childhood. As I lay there, I could feel a part of me that wanted to cry. But crying or making any outer noise was entirely foreign to me. Even though I wanted to move through this very uncomfortable place I was in, I had no outer ability to cry. My experience with crying was that it was dangerous. As a child, I had become very adept at trying to stay safe.

At some point in the experience, I was transported back in time, and I felt deep pain and age-old, brittle grief surfacing. Part of me knew this was the pain I had been avoiding at all costs because it seemed so deep and so horrible that it would kill me. I felt suspended between going where I never wanted to go and wanting to move through what I knew was stopping me from living openheartedly in my present life. My resistance was winning. Melisa kept gently nudging me and supporting me in going deeper. She asked me if there was a noise that matched what I was feeling. I resisted answering her.

I lost all sense of time and space. At some point, Melisa asked several other women who were mothers to join me on the horse blanket. One woman lay down and put her head next to my head. Another woman lay down with her back touching my back. I felt supported. Finally, a sound came bubbling up out of me. The noise shocked me.

When I later saw the movie *Till: Telling the Tragedy of Emmett Till*, and I heard Till's mother keening after her son's lynching in Mississippi in 1955, I realized that I had my own keening experience that day. Keening is a horrible, anguished sound. While I lay there on the ground reexperiencing my childhood wounds, Eddie got as close to me as he could from the other side of the fence. Melisa told me that he was very focused on me during my process of working through my resistance to feeling the pain I never wanted to feel.

Soon I was keening, similar to the sound the baby rabbit made when I was a little girl at the one-room schoolhouse. I felt into a deep wound inside that seemed so hurt and so sad about how I had been treated. I had entered a spiral of releasing emotions and feelings that were stuck deep inside me. I felt like I was in an altered state. Even though part of me was worried about what the others there might think of me, another part of me was observing this process and nudging me forward because I believed this experience would help me heal.

After what could have been several minutes or an eternity, I began to come back to being present in front of the round corral. I saw Eddie on the other side of the fence. Melisa asked me if I wanted to go into the round corral with Eddie. I pulled myself together because I really wanted to go to Eddie and experience my anchor, the love of a horse. Eddie immediately came to me and got as close to me as he could without stepping on me. He was very careful and soft. He nuzzled my face, heart area, and hands. As I walked slowly and quietly around, he followed me like a puppy. When I stopped, he wrapped his neck around me and gave me a full horse hug. I felt totally loved and present in a way that I had never experienced before in this life.

For the next few days of the training, I realized that I felt raw. Something big had shifted inside of me. I could feel that I had more tears to cry, but the dam inside that kept me from feeling the deep pain and sadness had broken. I knew I would not go back to the old me and that I would never be the same, in a good way.

Experiencing this session and the love and support from Eddie helped me transform a wound that had, until then, impacted how I experienced life. Now my wound seemed to be my portal to transformation, serenity, and greater freedom. By this, I mean that at a deep soul level, I felt freer and more connected to God and my husband and other loved ones than ever before.

After that experience, the trickle that had started inside me opened up into a greater flow of being able to feel and move through the pain, sadness, anger, and fear that had been blocking me from fully living. In addition to the weekend training sessions, I attended weekly classes, read multiple books, and practiced by phone different coaching skills with my classmates. One of the exercises that Melisa had each student work on was one to determine each of our core values. So, at the same time my defenses, restrictions, and the part of me that had built a wall to defend myself from being hurt were all melting, I was also determining what I knew about myself that was valuable. Through this self-exploration exercise, I realized what value was true north in my inner compass of being. One of my assignments was to determine my top four values, which was particularly difficult work. I persevered until I had my top twelve values articulated. Melisa taught us that our top three values rarely change, though the rest may change through the years of our life. The values exercise helped me to keep my eyes looking upward as I was shedding an outworn, restrictive consciousness that no longer served me.

A year later, I drove to attend another weekend training session. I drove halfway the first day and stayed in my horse trailer. On this trip, I had my three-year-old Gypsy/Shire mare Mystic with me, along with my cow dog Chewie. That evening, I stayed out in the middle of nowhere next to my friends' corral just south of the Canadian border. I felt deep, difficult emotions bubbling up inside. I felt like my throat was stuck and that I needed to let out these strange noises. Mystic stood with me as we watched the sun disappear, and I leaned against her and cried a little. But the feelings were stuck and could not seem to move on their own.

Once Mystic, Chewie, and I arrived at the arena, I got them each settled comfortably, and I attended the opening evening meeting of the several-day training session. Just like the year before, I again experienced deep emotions, fear, and discomfort in my body. As soon as the opportunity arose, I stepped forward to work with Melisa. Again, she said I would not need the microphone. Like before, my inner work that day was based on wounds from before I could talk. So that meant that my experience of and release of those stuck energies would not entail me using words.

Again, Melisa asked me to trust her. I chose to trust her because so far, she had acted trustworthy, and I knew I needed to heal from the deep pain I still had around my heart. She placed her chair behind me and asked me if it was okay for her to move her chair close behind me. I said yes. She moved in close, sitting behind me. She asked me if she could put her arms around me from behind me. I said yes. She was giving me a bear hug while sitting behind me with her arms around my shoulders.

As soon as she wrapped me up, I started crying in a way I had never cried before. Part of me wanted to run, but I did not want to break free from Melisa and hurt her. So I stayed put and surrendered to sobbing. Again, I lost time and space. I have no idea of most of what Melisa said. At some point, she said that if I wanted to, I could break free because I was stronger than her. This helped me stay and surrender to the healing process.

Just like the last time I experienced deep healing, for the next few days, I felt raw and somewhat discombobulated. My old ways of being were gone, but I had not yet integrated this new way of living true to my real self. I was stuck in the in-between place of no longer having my old patterns and habits of inner consciousness, but not yet having stepped into the new pattern of my soul living free in the here-and-now consciousness.

I remembered my beliefs about habits. I told myself that in twenty-one days, I would no longer even remember how uncomfortable I had felt after letting go of the way of being that no longer served me. Sometimes after doing a piece of work, I felt like someone had ripped an energetic scar off my energy system and the underlying wound had not yet been knitted together. In my mind, I visualized the angels knitting these parts of me back together with white light, creating a seamless white gown around me. Even though I could see the future wholeness around me, and I had experienced this healing process before, I still felt unbearably raw and vulnerable without my defenses. My focus on my values and looking up to the celestial realm to ask for the angels' assistance in sewing me back together in wholeness helped me make it through the many uncomfortable, somewhat painful times of the healing process.

After returning home to our ranch, one morning I was doing chores, feeding my horses, and pondering the whole process of creating good habits. I observed that once I started doing something at the same time each day, like feeding the horses or brushing my teeth, then after a few days, I would create an inner groove with outer actions that no longer required much thought. As I observed after developing a new habit, I became aware that I no longer needed to think about what to do next. Then, I realized that I was on the verge of developing a habit of being able to do things great and small with momentum and present awareness. It dawned on me what Jung meant when he discussed making the unconscious conscious.

Throughout my healing process in the training program, and even before, I had been experiencing deep, hidden feelings rising to the surface of my awareness. These were feelings that I had to die to be able to face, feel, and experience. Once I could feel and allow these feelings, memories, and experiences to move through me, that is when my unconscious became conscious. What was unconscious no longer acted like the submerged part of a big iceberg that could shipwreck me at any time. Instead, my ability to allow and experience these feelings opened my consciousness to more soul freedom.

I suspected the next step would be to create the habit of maintaining my consciousness and being in the free flow of feelings of deep peace, love, compassion, and the whole constellation of higher vibration consciousness that I can create. Then, after I have a habit of living in this new healthier, more whole inner and outer consciousness, when I drift into being unconscious, my habits will still carry me forward up the mountain of wholeness.

∞

CHAPTER 13

Keep Moving

∞

The pain of living
The pain of the Mother giving birth to an immortal consciousness
The pain that unites humanity in the embrace of life
The pain that cracks my heart open to be a vessel of light
The pain of the earth that so needs me to courageously feel

To say my path forward in transformational healing was arduous, an uphill climb, scary, and seemingly impossible is an understatement. When I promised God that I would do whatever it took to become whole, I had no idea the effort it would take. Many times, in moments when I lacked the courage and determination to carry on, I reminded myself of my promise to God. So, I kept moving forward, like climbing Mount Everest, one foot in front of the other. I knew that God would provide me with the support I needed when I needed it, so I just kept keeping on, no matter what.

For the first four to six months of 2016, all my efforts went toward finding a path forward for my physical body—my lungs and heart—to heal. We were still looking for the cause of the problem, so John and I decided we should go to the Mayo Clinic in Rochester, Minnesota. While filling out the paperwork, I spoke with my friend of more than twenty years who is a naturopathic doctor. When she heard of my plans to go to Mayo, she said that she had referred patients there before and that was a viable option. Yet, she was not positive that was what would be best for me. She pointed out that the best doctors in Montana had already worked my case, and it was highly likely the doctors at Mayo would run the same tests and get the same results—and it would cost more than one hundred thousand dollars. She suggested I first do some tests with a naturopathic doctor in Bozeman who specialized in mold exposure.

In February 2016, a blood test proved that my DNA had not provided me with the ability to handle mold exposure. We tested my office, my home in Bozeman, and my home at the ranch, which is where we found mold. So now we had the cause of the inflammation, and I started a protocol for prolonged mold exposure.

It is hard for me to remember much about this time because I still felt lousy. My body and being were so run down that I had very little energy, and part of my reaction to the mold was brain fog. I do remember that this period seemed to take forever. I laid around on the couch or in bed, something I had never done that many days in a row before. I was very frustrated because I did not feel like I was getting better, and I could not do very much. I did the bare minimum to run my law firm. I just did not feel good enough to do much work.

At times, I felt like giving up because it was so hard. I was not used to not being able to work, go outside, be with my horses, or go to the ranch on weekends. I felt depressed and anxious because I knew I had no control over the outcome. All I could do was be patient, pray to God, and follow the still, small voice when I felt led to follow a certain treatment plan—and ask for guidance along the way.

One of my naturopathic doctors suggested I seek out acupuncture treatments to assist my lungs and body in healing. I followed her direction and started seeing a local acupuncture practitioner weekly. At first, I could hardly drag myself to my appointments. As is usual with lung illness, I felt abnormally heavy in my body and my emotions. I was not ready to throw in the towel, but at many levels, I felt all effort was futile.

Gradually, I started having more energy and could sense the slow improvement. When she first started treating me, she would place the needles, leave the room, and then come back later to remove them. At some point, she asked me if I wanted her to stay in the room while the needles were doing their work. I followed my heart and answered yes. At this point, I had enough energy to observe myself observing her and our interaction. I realized that I could sense a vibrancy and way of being in her that I needed to learn from. She seemed to me like a willow tree, vibrant and full of resilience, yet very capable of moving with the winds of life.

I pondered how the healing in my body seemed like paying the mortgage on my house, like my payments were only going to interest and that I would never get out of debt, let alone get ahead financially. My inner awareness was that my health was so poor that the energy in my body was almost at a deficit. To heal, I needed to do whatever I could on the inner and outer to increase light energy in my body and being. I surrendered and followed my inner direction by keeping on, sometimes getting to celebrate a small victory with my health. At some point, everything changed, and not only was I out of debt, but I also had enough energy and health that it started compounding in my favor, just as a long-held property does once it has been paid off.

In addition to acupuncture, I took herbs and vitamins and followed the protocol for assisting my body in detoxifying from mold exposure created by one of my doctors, Dr. Schumacher. Though I was moving through healing my physical body, I still was experiencing disabling pain. At this point in my life, I had suffered from fibromyalgia, endometriosis, severe back pain, and migraine headaches for more than twenty years. I had had five surgeries for endometriosis, took so many over-the-counter anti-inflammatory drugs that I caused my kidneys to bleed, and had been prescribed painkillers, which I surrendered to taking because I could no longer function without them. Though I still suffered from chronic pain, I wished to no longer be taking painkillers to function.

Until I took the bar exam in 1995 and started working as a legal professional, I had been able to keep the trauma buried for almost thirty years. However, the extra professional responsibility and stress triggered what I later learned was PTSD. Once my body started running too many stress hormones due to PTSD, then I also developed chronic pain. In my experience, in addition to the stress, my pain was also caused by all the unexpressed emotions, including terror, simmering anger, and suppressed sadness from my childhood trauma. At a soul level, I never wanted to hurt anybody, so it seemed I held my emotions in and by doing this, I hurt myself.

During the many months I was moving through an intense journey of healing, I read all of Brené Brown's books, mostly on audio. In *Rising Strong*, Brown talks about reckoning with emotion and courageous behavior: "Emotion can feel terrible, even physically overwhelming. We can feel exposed, at risk, and uncertain in the midst of emotion."[24] Well, I certainly wanted to be courageous as I was seeking wholeness, coming back from an illness and chipping away at an energy deficit so great that it was only by grace that I was able to be filled with light gradually. I brought my feelings to light, was honest and curious, and chose to move through the portal of my pains that led to transformation and healing of old wounds.

This was around the time that one of my naturopathic doctors suggested I see Heidi Soper, who was trained to help the body release trauma. It was Bessel van der Kolk who first discussed this concept in his book, *The Body Keeps the Score*. In that book, van der Kolk offered a whole new paradigm for healing.[25] At this point in my healing, I knew nothing about his book, but because of my promise to God, I followed my doctor's directions and I started seeing Heidi. For almost two years I thought I would lose my mind as we worked together to help me release the unresolved trauma energy stored inside me. I would see her regularly, and sometimes I would call and get in on an urgent basis because whatever was happening inside me was too painful or overwhelming for me to be able to handle. So, I would ask her for help. Even as I was asking her for help, I also knew her work with me was stirring things up that terrified me.

At some point in the process, I realized that I wanted to stop taking the pain meds I had been taking for more than a decade. The mere act of reaching out and asking for help allowed me to deal with the pain. I decided to experiment and see whether I could change my inner and outer dependence on the meds. I told myself that I could change everything about myself—how my body functioned, how I responded to pain, my emotional state, and more—because these were all energetic habits. I knew that I could change any habit if I could do something different for twenty-one days. I decided to use bodywork and my relationship with my therapists and doctors to try another method of dealing with pain. It did not happen overnight, but amazingly, I did stop needing pain meds. And even without pain meds, I am pain-free today. Nobody on my team of doctors and other medical practitioners expected I would ever be completely pain-free. It is a bit of a miracle.

One day when things got hard, I tried to gently keep all my four lower bodies—the physical, mental, emotional, and spiritual—in my chair, focusing on the tasks at hand. But that was not working. I finally had to break free and go out into Mother Nature. At first, as I was walking outside, my consciousness was still bouncing around in my head. It is a wonder I could walk with as little attention as I put into my physical body. All of a sudden, I heard the birds. Oh my, what a beautiful song they were singing! As I listened to the birds, all of me dropped into my body, and I truly appreciated being here now. Now I could see the path clearly in front of me, pointed up the hill. Even though I thought I had waited to go out until the spring storms had gone away, it was not long before the rain and sleet came down, and I was soaked. But I was not going to stop. I strongly wanted to get up that hill so I could meet up with my horses.

At the top, Mystic came running. She thundered toward me, and I wondered if she would stop. She did, and I put the halter on her and started my descent with Mystic in tow. Even though she is fairly well-trained, she balked and did not want to leave her herd. She did not want to leave the grass and freedom that she had roaming those high hills. Several times, she even planted her hooves and resisted any forward movement. I talked to her and reminded her that I was the leader of our team. She still did not want to obey and leave her herd on the high plains.

The lesson is that just like Mystic, parts of me on the inner and the outer sometimes do not want to move forward. Yet, my higher self (that is often my leader) reminds me that if I do not move forward to finish a project, I will not get paid. I will not succeed at achieving my goals. So even when I do not want to leave the herd of my friends or when I would rather play than work, I surrender and move forward.

I told Mystic that I would return her to the herd in several days, and between now and then we were going to work together on some training. If I never asked Mystic to leave her herd and work with me, we would never develop our relationship, and she would not learn the skills for being a good horse partner. When I move forward, even when I do not want to, I develop the skills and strength to climb my inner and outer mountains.

I realized that for me to make transformational inner and outer changes, I needed to change my habits. In the past when I had focused on changing my habits, I tried to use force on myself. When I felt I was overweight, like many, I would put myself on a rigid diet—which never worked. In fact, nothing I have tried to change about myself using rigid force has been successful. In addition to treating myself with compassion, I also became aware that I had to be a gentle supportive leader to create change.

Mystic and other horses do not trust a human unless the human embodies compassion and leadership. A horse is a prey animal and naturally uses its flight-or-fight consciousness for survival. I became aware in the process of working with Mystic and other horses that my soul is similar to a horse.

In addition to furthering my understanding of compassion, Mystic also taught me a very valuable lesson about my inner misuse of power. One time, she and I were at a natural horsemanship clinic where most of the other horses were of a smaller, athletic Quarter Horse type. Mystic is almost sixteen hands tall and weighs around sixteen hundred pounds. She is a big girl.

At the clinic, the teacher had us do these exercises to show how flexible and soft our horses were. At that time, I was not soft and flexible on the inside. I had flashed back into my competitive self and instead of being present with Mystic, I was observing the others in the class and comparing myself and Mystic to them. I wanted to be the best, and I wanted Mystic to react and turn like those little horses in the class. Instead of being a good, soft leader for Mystic, I resorted to jamming her. Now, I was not jerking or spurring her. But one can jam another part of life, or even ourselves, without leaving outer signs. I was jamming her with my energy.

Mystic, like many Gypsies, is extremely sensitive. One of my teachers jokingly told me she thought Gypsy horses were only one DNA strand away from being embodied fairies. Mystic is also incredibly smart and kind. She did not react to me by acting out. She simply graciously ignored my increasingly forceful, demanding energy. The more she ignored me, the more I felt frustrated inside, and the more I increased my age-old strategy of misusing power. At the time, I had no awareness that my habit increased my outer problems.

The teacher gently asked if she could ride my horse. I said, "Of course," got off Mystic, and handed her the reins. Before she got on Mystic, the teacher gently pulled on the reins from each side to see if Mystic would give to pressure. As soon as Mystic would give to pressure, the teacher would release. Mystic responded as though she understood and liked this communication. Unlike the teacher, I had just increased pressure, failing to give Mystic any release for trying to respond to my request.

After Mystic and the teacher had established their connection and communication through those ground exercises, the teacher got on Mystic. She rode Mystic around and within a few minutes, Mystic was responding and moving softly like a ballerina. Granted, she still did not move quickly, which is what I had been trying to force her to do. My desire for her to move fast was only to fulfill my ego and desire to show off. The class was about natural horsemanship, which entails the horse moving with oneness, softness, and connection with the rider.

After the teacher dismounted and I was riding Mystic back to our trailer during the lunch break, it seemed that Mystic told me that the problem we had been having was not her fault. Humbly, I had to agree with her because I had witnessed how she was with the teacher. My new awareness was that I had an inner habit of misusing force on myself as well as in outer situations to try to get what I wanted. I also realized that this habit never worked out for the better.

I really started making progress on my path to wholeness when I started treating all parts of myself as I treated my horses. I love my horses. My horses have always been an open portal to higher dimensions, and when I am with them, I feel grounded to the earth and open to the heavens.

Also, as I opened to loving parts of myself and loved myself as I did my horses, my horses opened their hearts and connected in greater ways to me. This process also opened me to greater connection with people. As I observed myself becoming more able to give and receive love, I also observed that part of my need for pain meds was to fill the empty hole in my heart. During my therapy with Lucile, I told her that I realized that I had been living with a torturous feeling of a gaping wound inside me that could not be filled from the outside or inside. I shared with her the realization this was the underlying core feeling, the pain of lack, that I tried to mute with alcohol, drugs, and overworking. I explained that my love of horses seemed to bypass my defenses to help heal the hole inside me. I also felt like, in the presence of horses, the angels could work to sew up those jagged parts of me that had been wounded.

Early on in my spiritual studies, I came across the teaching that there is no injustice. I had a hard time digesting that concept—it seemed to me that injustice was all around. Why was I abused as a little girl? How could that not be injustice? My mom choked me. What could I have done at four or five years old to deserve that? Since I could not square that teaching with my life experience, I decided to wait and see if I gained more awareness and a greater understanding around it.

At some point in my healing, I became more and more aware that my early childhood trauma had set me up for being able to choose life instead of death when I was out of my body. This was in part thanks to my psychology—the creation of my unreal self while experiencing life with a body on Earth. This self-created, unreal self blocked me from being able to identify with my real self as I was created by God.

One time during counseling, I told Lucile that I was resilient. She said I had never said that before. Also, she asked if I ever felt like a victim. I pondered her statement and question and answered, "No, I had not felt like a victim." What came to me was that my life had been like a leppy calf. *Leppy* is another word for "orphan." When a calf is orphaned and has no mother, the other cows do not usually let the leppy calf drink milk from their udders. Nature has programmed the cows to take care of their own calves, which we believe they know primarily by the sense of smell. If a mother cow fed every calf that came by in a five-hundred-cow herd, she would not only run out of milk for her calf, but it would also upset the order of the herd. In a herd of mother cows, each cow feeds their own calf.

For a leppy calf to get to drink milk, the calf has to be persistent, insistent, and resilient against rejection. The leppy calf has to be willing to compete with the calf that belongs to the cow and to keep trying one cow after another until it can bum some milk. Also, the leppy calf starts eating grass and does whatever it takes to survive. The leppy calf does not expect that any cow is going to take care of it.

As I look back at my childhood, it seems that for me to be able to achieve what I need to in this life, I needed my mom in her humanness. Sometimes, I believe she overplayed her role and went for the Emmy instead of just playing her role adequately. Apparently, I needed my difficult childhood to find my resilience, strength, and courage to ask the Divine Mother for nourishment for my soul. Sure, my childhood could have been easier, but an easy life does not create the inner dynamics to strive and move forward no matter what happens.

I identify with being a leppy soul, who, during her mid-fifties, finally found enough courage to ask for nourishment. Until dying, I was more afraid of getting hurt and rejected than I was of my soul starving. Also, I believed I could take care of myself by being tough and using my extreme willpower. I never wanted to depend on anybody, even a mother figure, for anything. After leaving my body and then returning, I was no longer afraid of dying. Instead, I became more afraid of not living.

To be obedient to God and get into my body and find wholeness, I had to seek, ask, and then rely on multiple women in various healing professions to assist me on my healing path. This was the hardest thing I had ever done. As a child, I found ways to survive, but I never fully trusted a woman to support and help me. My recourse was to run away with my horses to find safety. Now, to heal, I had to learn to trust and allow others to closely connect with me.

Looking back, I realize that if I had not allowed Mother to hug me all those years ago, I probably would not have been able to endure the inner terror and turmoil that surfaced during these healing sessions with the lovely team of women that I found in Bozeman to assist in my healing path. Before dying, my psychology would not have allowed me to open my heart and receive the support I needed to heal.

At this stage in my life, I still do not fully understand the concept that there is no injustice. Yet, my life experience and my ability to choose life over death bring me the awareness that every challenge in my life seems to set me up for forging a hard-won victory. I truly believe that everything I have experienced was a stepping stone to where I am today.

For example, if my mom had been a perfect mother, I probably would not have been so hungry to develop a relationship with God and the Divine Mother. Had I not been a leppy soul, I would not have had the soul wounds that compelled me forward to search for inner and outer wholeness. I am certain that there is divine order in my life, and I'm grateful that I have moved through the many challenges necessary to overcome my lesser self. Also, part of me believes that I have lived before and sown the seeds that resulted in my choosing my mom for this life.

Even though my childhood instilled deep wounds of terror, pain, and sadness inside me, I always loved my mom. My desire to save her was not healthy and probably would be called *enmeshment* in psychological terms. Much of my mind and heart were constantly filled with my desire to see her heal. I had even experimented with saying violet flame decrees for more than three hours, invoking light for her healing. I was obsessed with my deep desire to see her heal.

She waited for me to join my two brothers and sister at her side before she died. I prayed for her safe journey in her transition from her body. I told her she could go and that I loved her.

I am sure that if I had not had the experience of my mom, I would not be the person I have become. I have even found gratitude because of the deep well of love and wholeness I now have to share with others. By grace, I have been able to heal the inner wound that she could not heal in her lifetime.

Even though I do not fully understand why the leaders in my church wanted to hurt me, I also made peace with their actions. The truth is, I do not know what was going on in their world and what they thought they were trying to do. In her book, Brown asked her husband if he believes everybody is trying to do their best.[26] Since he is an introvert, he pondered this and answered a few days later. He told her that he believed everyone did their best because he realized that was the best he could do for himself. I choose to believe that my parents did the best they could. Also, looking back, I realize that the pain I felt in response to their actions was the catalyst to move me closer to oneness with God.

Sage, my young palomino Gypsy/Quarter Horse cross, attended a horsemanship clinic with me, and he was one of my teachers there. By nature, he is very sweet, inquisitive, innocent, and a bit precocious. Sage has never had trauma and shows up with an open mind and heart. I learned that when I engage with Sage with true embodied confidence and compassion, he would do anything I asked. But I had to communicate clearly and use his language.

Horses are in constant communication with each other, but they do not use words. Horses embody their thoughts and emotions, using their bodies to communicate with each other. In some ways, their communication seems clearer and cleaner than that of humans. We use words that are often not congruent with our feelings. And when we communicate that way, it is ineffective—both for horses and humans.

Sage taught me to whisper to him, being fully present, clear in my intent, and, most importantly, totally congruent to my own peaceful center of being. He let me be his leader because he trusted me, and he gave me his trust because I was worthy. We shared the slice-of-heaven connection that occurs when two lives communicate with trust and compassion.

My experience with Sage reminded me that my healing path had truly started when I began treating myself with the leadership and compassion I shared with my horses. As I was climbing out of the abyss of my inner fragmentation at multiple levels of being, I treated myself as I would a young colt in training. I became patient and kind to myself. When I am training a colt, I reward any effort to move forward in the right direction. I decided that self-condemnation and self-criticism could not exist in my round corral of healing. When my

PTSD was triggered and my inner being bolted, I tried to keep from startling further or tightening up. I strove to keep myself calm and stroked my inner being with a soothing energy, just like I would my horse. I told myself I was no longer in trauma. I was safe.

Just like training Sage, it took time for my inner being to shift when I whispered to my soul with kindness. I knew that Sage and all other young horses I have trained take a certain amount of time and repetition to learn and trust that they are not going to be hurt or asked to do something that will harm them. My inner being was the same.

Mystic and Sage taught me that I have a part of myself that can rise to higher consciousness and whisper to lead all my wounded parts home. I sometimes ponder that this leader in us is similar to Christ and is the true leader of our hearts. Just as Sage, Mystic, and other horses can immediately sense if I am congruent and whispering to them clearly from a point of compassionate leadership, my soul also knows whether it can trust the part of me that is leading.

I have always wanted to be a better horse whisperer and have an ongoing enlightened partnership with all horses. Now, I want to be a better soul whisperer to provide loving leadership in drawing all parts of myself home to my heart. I truly believe that the best way for me to change the world around me is to follow my healing path and embody as much wholeness as I can contain. And I believe that wholeness is mysticism minus mystique. Wholeness is oneness with my divine pattern and my reason for being.

There is no doubt that to discover true healing we each need grit. Even the word *grit* is included in the word *integrity*.

That hospital-bed promise to God to do whatever was needed to heal and accomplish my reason for being, along with my internal dedication to integrity and honor have been the grit for years of deep healing. Without them, I am not sure I would have had enough humbleness and integrity to learn lessons from my horses. This process of healing and facing my bad habits has been more difficult than winning state championships, succeeding in law school, or developing an accomplished small business. It took all my grit and understanding to learn from Mystic and Sage so I could follow through on addressing my areas inside that lacked integration with the divine.

∞

CHAPTER 14

Who I Think I Am Matters

∞

One day, I rode Mystic and noticed she had this restriction when I asked her to flex or give in to my right rein. My first impulse was to kick her with my right leg and, as a cowboy would, force her into giving. How do you think that worked, with her big strong workhorse build? She reinforced the lesson that no part of life can force another part of life into being flexible or giving to pressure. My use of pressure caused Mystic to double down on her resistance.

Soon, my trainer got on Mystic and experimented with various ways to help her find her true nature, which wanted to partner and connect with her rider. He did not use force like I had tried when riding her. He was asking her to put her weight on her hind left hock, which used to hurt her. Her mind told her it was going to hurt. She resisted, even though that was not her true nature. He continued to experiment with ways to help her understand that all he was asking was that she give to pressure. Soon, she chose the right answer. As soon as she gave to pressure, my trainer released it, which was her reward. Mystic figured it out, and she found the groove of nonresistance. Her whole being flowed with an elegant softness. Even though she is a big horse, she moved like a dancer.

As I observed her work through her resistance, I realized my work was very similar. I, too, would rather exist in connection and flow with others. I, too, have tangles, memories of pain, and blocked energy that tell me I cannot give in to pressure because I am avoiding whatever has been stuck in that tangle. Mystic was sure it would hurt her hock, and when it did not, she was surprised. I, too, have thought it would hurt me to move through my blockages.

Mystic did not enjoy every moment of her ride that night. But she stayed engaged with an open heart as she struggled to find the right answer. Ultimately, she found a flow and seemed to be freer in her connection with the trainer and me. She showed me how to persist in working through resistance. To not get frustrated or belligerent. To keep trying even though it can be hard to find one's way to freedom through our built-in resistance. It was so amazing to see how moving through the resistance quickly allowed her to find a fluidity and agility one would not believe could exist in a mare her size.

On my last training weekend in the Equine Gestalt program, I took along Mystic and my other horse, Captain. Mystic was four years old at the time, which is not old enough to coach yet. We wait until the horses have reached a bit of maturity and have been around people a lot—typically age five. During the twelve-hour drive from our home in Montana to the ranch in Colorado, I was pondering how much had shifted inside me and how much freer I felt. I was even cocky enough to think that maybe I did not have any work left to do. Part of me laughed at that thought because I knew that my embodiment of wholeness will always leave room for further growth.

Upon arriving at the ranch, I was already a little emotional because my two-year journey to learn the Equine Gestalt Coaching Method was coming to an end. I had grown to love the program, my classmates, my mentor Melisa, and the whole process of finding wholeness inside myself so I could assist others on their path to wholeness. Even though I had spent more than thirty-five years on a devoted spiritual path before I started working with horses in this way, I still felt like I needed the safety of the coaching program, my community of students, and Melisa's guidance to navigate the parts of my unreal self that blocked me from embodying my divine self.

I observed the other students working with Melisa and the student coaches to experience something from their past, giving them a choice of whether they wanted to allow their past to affect their lives in the present time. At one point, I started feeling very uncomfortable in my body. I could not sit still. I found myself pacing the back of the indoor arena until it was my turn to take the hot seat and one of my classmates, Evie Rose, started coaching me.

She asked if I would go get one of the stuffed teddy bears from where they were stored. I blurted, "I am not going to touch that teddy bear." My friend looked at me a little shocked. She had never heard me talk or act like that before—it was as though I had no filter. All of a sudden, I shifted and gave full embodiment to a part of me that had been hurt when I was a little girl. This part was tough and had decided that I was never going to be hurt again.

This part of me would do whatever it took to protect me, including trying to block me from feeling vulnerable. Melisa, who was sitting behind me, realized that my friend was in trouble, so she assisted in coaching from behind me. I could hear Melisa and Evie Rose yammering at me—at least that is what it sounded like to me, because of the state of consciousness I had adopted. My attorney training jumped to the forefront of my mind, and I wanted to eviscerate both Evie Rose and Melisa with my words. I sat there in my chair, refusing to do what Evie Rose asked. It was as if my mind was on steroids, flipping through what words I could use to hurt Evie Rose and get Melisa to back off. But I chose not to voice these words because even though that part of me was on a rampage, and the part was familiar, I did not identify with it as my real self.

The part of me that wanted to strike out against Evie Rose and Melisa was not consistent with how I identified with who I was spiritually. For a time, I felt like I was an observer of the process. I felt the unfolding of this underlying part of me that had made decisions about how it would protect me from harm, this part of me that advocated for aggressive action and words to keep Evie Rose and Melisa away from me. Instead, I listened to another part of me that thought an aggressive reaction was not necessary based on my experience of them. This other part did not believe that Evie and Melisa wanted to hurt me.

Mystic was in the round corral to help me. She had been given a special dispensation to partner with Evie Rose to coach me since she was my horse, even though she was young. While making this allowance, none of us could have realized how important Mystic's love and support would be to help me.

Time and space ceased to exist for me. I felt like I existed in the past and the present, and I could feel multiple layers of myself all converging together. At some point, I saw and felt Mystic's presence near me. She was standing as close to me as she could despite the fence that separated us. I looked into her eye, and I felt her big, supportive heart and love for me. Melisa reminded me that this was my final training weekend and therefore my last opportunity to move through this stuck place inside me. That statement softened me some, but I was not yet ready to comply with Melisa and Evie Rose. Then Melisa said, "Come on, you are boring me." I almost blew a cork when she said that. Instead, I stayed in the observing place, and I did not act on the rage that was coming up inside me. It dawned on me, based on my spiritual understanding, that my holding onto or grasping this angry, tough shell was in itself grounds for much of my suffering and inability to heal.

In the course, Melisa taught us that the body speaks first during the healing process. So, I reached over to pick up the teddy bear and sarcastically said, "The body speaks first." Once I had the bear in my lap, my body did speak first. I collapsed into tears over the bear and released the harsh shell. I had never let that part of me surface and talk before. But it was so foundational to my underbelly that it often drove me in all areas of my life. All else that I had done to heal my inner self had been leading up to this moment.

Instead of being driven by my consciousness or the parts that lived beneath my outer awareness, I experienced the pain, the agony, and the fear of being hurt, and I felt the love and admiration I had for Melisa and Evie Rose. Prior to this session, throughout those first intense years of healing, I had numerous disturbing dreams. Some had included male gangsters dressed in black clothes who broke into my house and chased me through the many rooms of a large house. Sometimes, in these ongoing dreams, they just chased me, and sometimes they captured me. Sometimes I fought back and escaped. I was sure these intruders wanted to hurt and kill me.

Another one of my recurring dreams was about a huge, Jabba the Hutt–like monster that lived in the room down the hall from me. This monster was tied up in chains, and sometimes I could hear him fighting against them. When he fought, he made the whole world rumble and shake. In my dreams, I wanted to stay away from this monster and would tremble with fear even when I knew he was locked in chains in his room—it never seemed to be enough to constrain him.

I had a similar dream one night, but it seemed like I was in a minimum-security prison where I could roam around outside my room. The most significant part of this dream was that I heard a prisoner in the room next door roaring and struggling against the chains that bound him. In my mind, I thought the prisoner was a murderer imprisoned one cell away from me, and I didn't want to have anything to do with the guy. But I did not have intense feelings during the dream, just concern for my safety because my cell door was open all the time. But I decided that because he was locked up, he could not come into my cell even though he was next door.

Another night I dreamt that I got a new house, but I had not moved in yet. The house had many rooms and was built with fine craftsmanship. I remember that the home was located at a high elevation, as well as in a holy place. I was inside the house and men were chasing me, but they could not reach me in this house.

I had built a structure of defenses, patched together based on decisions I made when I was four or five that I was never going to let anybody hurt me again. My experience was that every healing shift that occurred after bodywork with Heidi would be followed by an inner emotional fear, anxiety, anger, or some other flare. Likewise, my work with Lucile sparked an inner shift that would sometimes trigger a pain or place in my body that was stuck.

For example, if Heidi did any work around my neck, I would immediately feel terror, and I would flashback to my mom choking me. So I would follow Heidi and try to stay in my body instead of disassociating. She would ask what I felt, and if I answered with an emotion, she affirmed that and then asked what I felt in my body. She then would ask where in my body did I feel whatever I was feeling. My experience was that once I focused on my body, I could tolerate the flurry of emotions that arose. True, I sometimes felt physical discomfort—even pain. But even though the whole healing process pushed me to the end of my ability to tolerate discomfort and pain, I could tell that the light within my body was starting to move.

There is no linear way to explain the healing process because, for me, I truly experienced what some have called the peeling of the onion. Once I had done the somatic experiencing work with Heidi and counseling with Lucile, the healing modality of the Equine Gestalt Coaching Method seemed to be the final input that helped my defenses melt. If one layer of my defenses or false identity was transformed, then my whole inner and outer world also shifted.

Gradually, I noticed that I no longer had the dream about the men dressed in black chasing me. At some point in the process of healing, I did go into the monster's room in my dream and expected to see this huge blob of a thing waiting to break loose and kill me, but all I saw there were the chains. It was as though the monster had melted away into nothing and no longer existed. I was so surprised to see him gone. I sometimes wondered if the monster was a personification of my unreal self that I created by weaving together my defenses.

During this period of healing, I increased my spiritual practice and regularly gave fifteen minutes to an hour and a half of prayers, decrees, or meditation every morning. My inner prompting told me that for me to heal, I had to invoke light through spoken prayer or decrees. I used my ability to focus to slow my mind down to visualize that for which I was praying.

Similarly, my experience with Mystic in the round corral after my deep processing coaching session with Evie Rose and Melisa seemed to free me from those unconscious terrors and nightmares. After this, I knew I wanted to coach others—with the help of my horses—to assist them on the healing path to wholeness. Mystic helped me make that choice as she supported me fully that day.

Driving home from that final teaching, I realized I would never be the same again. I felt so grateful for the opportunity to grow and heal and amazed at how free I felt at a soul level. I also felt incredibly vulnerable, as I had let go of a restriction in my energy field that I had wrongly thought would protect me. But I knew, from forming other habits in my healing experience, that in twenty-one days, I would no longer be aware of the discomfort I felt during the drive home. Again, I remembered what I had learned as a little girl chasing cows—that pretty soon this uncomfortable part of my life would be over, and I would be drinking hot chocolate in front of the fireplace, so to speak.

In my Gestalt Coaching training, we learned that the body speaks first. Kelly McDaniel wrote, "Your body is simply biologically wired in protective mode and responds very quickly, below your awareness, to anything that is a reminder of childhood abuse. In other words, you don't 'choose' a reaction that may be extreme or frightening to yourself and others. Your response is automatic and somatic (based in the body)."[27]

McDaniel also wrote, "I don't consider Third-Degree Mother Hunger a disorder; it's a profound attachment injury that creates a constellation of symptoms that make life unbearable."[28] Certainly, for more than fifty years of my life, I felt that life was unbearable due to the weight of sadness, grief, and deep pain. Finally, after many years of pursuing a spiritual practice and inner and outer healing, I was at a place where I was ready to stop being someone other than my true self. I had known on the outer that each of us, including me, was made in a unique divine pattern by God. I knew that just like snowflakes, no two souls were identical. I knew I had my own divine geometrical pattern of consciousness and identity in divine oneness.

Also, I knew that, throughout my being and consciousness, I had energy tangles that kept the light from flowing through me. At one point I wrote a poem:

I am an instrument of my Father in heaven
As if I were a flute
No, this flute is not perfectly pitched, as of yet
He blows into this instrument
At times the melody comes out harmoniously
At times it is out of tune, or off-key
It always seems that as soon as one song is perfected
He changes the music
Then many discordant noises come out of this flute
Now, a flute is made to release beautiful music
However, it is the practice of the scales
That results in perfect harmonious notes
When will the flute release only perfect music
It seems my Father is continually writing new music
I suppose this flute will always be striving
For the perfection of beautiful music unto God

Every time I go within and experience and then transform one of these tangles where my true identity is blocked, I am becoming more of my divine identity embodied. To shed and then transform the tangle, I found that I needed to invoke light through prayer, meditation, and other means to raise my vibration.

A real transformative change occurred when I felt the experience of the tangle and simultaneously held invocations to God in my consciousness. For example, after one of these training weekends when I experienced so much physical release of restrictions, I dipped pretty low upon returning home. I could feel this deep well of emotional pain and overwhelming sadness. I felt very uncomfortable emotionally and sick to my stomach. At first, I wanted to avoid these feelings by being busy, watching TV, or drinking something to numb the pain, but I knew these were not the ways to move through this. I felt overwhelmed, and I thought of reaching out to call somebody to help talk me through this deep anguish.

My inner prompting was to lie down in my bed, curl up in the fetal position and surrender to feeling the pain. While I was lying there, I spoke the violet flame mantra, "I am a being of violet fire, I am the purity God desires," over and over. Also, in my mind's eye, I visualized my pain being consumed in a violet-looking fire. Soon, I felt extremely hot all over my body, and the deep, dark emotional and physical feelings shifted and resolved. I felt like these feelings I had so long wanted to avoid simply melted away by my practice of being able to experience the pain and focus on the light at the same time. I was no longer burdened with the negative thoughts that used to accompany the pain.

This was a huge turning point in my transformational healing path because instead of applying my prayer ritual in an outer, sometimes rote, manner, I made the inner connection to experiencing the light through invocation in my physical and emotional bodies. Looking back, it seems so simple that invoking light through the science of the spoken word would lead to healing in multiple layers of my being.

Prior to invoking light and experiencing the heat and transformation inside myself, I operated with a compartmentalized being. I had studied the sacred science of alchemy and understood the possibility of transforming the base qualities of my human nature into a higher consciousness while here on Earth. In their book on alchemy, the Prophets said, "the conscious invocation of Life makes all of the alchemist's manifestations doubly secure."[29]

Finally, after many years of studying and applying prayer and mantra in my daily life, I started to embody the inner meaning of alchemy, which according to the Prophets is "all-composition, implying the relation of the all of the creation to the parts that compose it. Thus alchemy . . . is the science of the mystic and it is the forte of the self-realized man who, having sought, has found himself to be one with God, and is willing to play his part."[30] I became aware of my oneness with God, and I was willing to play my part on Earth.

∞

CHAPTER 15

Being Me Now

∞

Oh, the jagged rawness of pain and the trickle of light that flows from the sun to awaken the spring of life
Through portals of pain, we connect, unite, and give birth to a new way of living that raises Mother Earth and life into Light
I felt the deep caverns of endless pain chasing me
I struggled to avoid falling into the abyss of deep pain
I turned and faced the Light
I felt my pain
I felt my mother's pain
I felt others' pain
I felt the Earth's pain
My heart cracked open and more Light came in
My heart is growing in love, mercy, and compassion
Joy follows in the footsteps of the portal of pain

When I first got serious about my healing path, I was in a deep hole of a health deficit. All four of my lower bodies were sick in multiple ways. My physical body had shut down due to extreme inflammation. My mental body was in a habit of running defensive maneuvers to keep me from being hurt as I had been in my childhood. My emotional body was one hundred percent engaged in fight, flight, or freeze mechanisms because of unresolved trauma. Spiritually, I attempted to disconnect from the other three bodies because I just wanted to go home to God. Just like paying my mortgage, when I started my healing climb, I could barely scrape enough healing energy to pay the interest necessary for my ongoing maintenance of myself.

Even though the task of healing seemed impossible, I trusted that God had not allowed me to come back to simply suffer. I trusted that if I were obedient to my inner direction and gave everything I had, something would shift. Invoking light through a devotional practice opened my consciousness to learning how to embody light. I discovered that any place within my four lower bodies and consciousness that was not in alignment with my divine geometry actively resisted embodying light and love. I learned to trust the process and that my resistances and defenses were no longer necessary. When I could withstand the discomfort of fear, pain, vulnerability, and other feelings I usually tried to avoid, I found relief in prayer. I felt something being transformed inside of myself.

There is a place deep inside each of our hearts where we connect with God. This place is physical but also of other dimensions. I say it is physical because our spiritual connection lives within our physical heart. In this place, I am safe with God from all that happens in our outer worlds. When I am deeply connected in this place, I can serve God in heaven and on Earth and be an anchor point for God's light to work miracles on Earth.

I discovered that the key to entering and staying in this secret chamber of my heart is love. Only love will allow me to move through to the impervious protection barricading this spot located deep within my heart. This is a love that transcends my human form and limitations. This is a love that carried me inward and upward to total connection with God—as above, so below.

This love is attainable through resolving my emotional defenses, wounds, or whatever else creates a feeling of separation from God. Once I moved through the portals of pain—each of these places in my consciousness that once created a feeling of separation or duality—then I began to find more wholeness, oneness, and nonduality. I began to experience moments of flowing in the stream of God's consciousness.

At some point on the path to wholeness, I began to be more aware that I am a molecule in the ocean of God's love. At this point, I no longer felt alone at sea, for now, I was one with the sea. Pursuing wholeness by courageously moving through the portals of pain has brought me closer to finding inner peace. Many of my feelings of separation have evaporated, and sometimes all that remains is being in one vibration with God's love.

Before I graduated from my Equine Gestalt Coaching course in 2020, I held my first retreat for five women who had all lost someone to suicide. As I was preparing for this three-day retreat at our ranch, I went through cycles of feeling insecure, like I could not assist these women on their healing path. One day I was having a bit of a meltdown with thoughts of how I would not be enough, so I communicated with Melisa. She reminded me that my coaching at the retreat was not about me and that I had just spent two years learning what I needed to know to partner with my horses and help these women. Most importantly, she told me that she believed in me. Melisa often told us to "trust the process."

Instead of allowing my fears, insecurities, and non-belief in myself to run me ragged, I slowed myself down and decided to stay focused on the present moment. I relaxed into finishing the multitude of things that need to be done to provide food, housing, and coaching to the five women who were arriving at our ranch. I had purchased several gifts for each of them, and I decided I would open my heart and meet each person where they were with no expectations and no judgment. Once the women started to arrive, I immediately moved into a sweet zone of being that I had just barely touched before this retreat.

Early on in the training program, I felt I was too busy with my law practice to truly focus on learning the intellectual part of the training. I decided what I did have the capacity to focus on was becoming anchored in my heart to create a safe place for whoever was sitting with me and my horses for coaching. I went deep into my heart and found a place where I felt very vertically connected to the Divine. I tapped into this connection in my heart to be fully present and to hear and see fully the women as they entered places they had been avoiding since their loved ones' suicides. I realized that my role was to connect as openly and deeply as possible with each client because that connection is ground zero for their healing journey. This allowed me to join my clients as they traveled their inner and outer experiences of their pain. I witnessed my clients enter what at first must have seemed like a great chasm between their present and experiencing feelings that they had been avoiding for decades. I witnessed the women embrace the process with courage and let go of grief, pain, sadness, and whatever else no longer served them. They each did courageous Gestalt work and experienced the healing love of my horses.

Buddy was with me for my first retreat at the old age of thirty-three, which is somewhat equivalent to being in his mid-nineties if he were a human. Tears ran down my cheeks several times during that retreat because I knew Buddy would not be with me much longer. Having him with me as I completed the circle—from him telling me to open my heart and trust others to this moment, where I was moved to open my heart even further—was so profound. He stayed with me all those years to help me live my reason for being. Buddy worked with clients that first weekend, and I felt so blessed to have him there with me, my heart horse. Buddy is now gone, though I continue, nourished by the gifts he gave me.

Before that weekend, I had never maintained a vertical connection to God as continuously as I did at the retreat serving those women. My focus on maintaining that connection helped me find the freest, purest consciousness I have ever maintained for a prolonged period. I now know that giving everything I have to serve others transforms my life. Finding more wholeness created a consciousness of freedom throughout my being.

Going through all that I did in this life had to happen so I could be the me of today and serve others on their path to wholeness. If I had not struggled with my mom and her suicide threats and dealt with my own suicidal ideation at times, I would not have been prepared to be fully present with those women when they first experienced the feelings they had been suppressing.

In the West, we are trained by the outer environment to believe that our only body is our physical body. I have experienced that I have three other bodies—my spiritual, emotional, and mental bodies. Sometimes, I ponder about what a "body" is. To me, a body is an organization of energy or light that is unique to each person. So we each have a fire or spiritual body where our energy or atomic frequency is the highest because it is closest to our divine identity. This body enshrines our God potential and cradles our souls. This etheric body also stores the memories of all our experiences.

As I have mentioned, when I was pursuing deep healing, in my inner world, I saw my four horses. I experienced my spiritual horse, the white stallion, as not being able to partner with my other three horses because he was free and lived in higher vibrational awareness. In some ways, my spiritual horse existed in my consciousness like a mystical unicorn that sometimes was visible through the mist but was not anchored or united with the rest of me.

During my healing, I created my logo for my life work, Four Horses for Wholeness, in honor of the four horses of my four lower bodies (the white stallion, the bay stallion, the palomino mare, and the draft cross mare). It also honors the four outer horses who came into my life while I was healing.

Starting on the left is Ruby, a bay Thoroughbred and Quarter Horse cross mare that I rescued from a boring life of being a trail horse. She loves to chase cows on the ranch. When Ruby began coaching, she realized she had a special gift and seemed to be amazed that she could help people heal. She brings her lead mare personality of taking care of the herd into her coaching work. In my inner being, Ruby symbolizes my emotional body. She is sensitive, a little hot-blooded, and sometimes throws short, intense tantrums, but she loves to keep moving forward. Ruby can be extremely compassionate and willing to be still and stay with someone who is courageously facing their inner pain.

Next to Ruby is Mystic. She found me at an Amish auction when she was three. Mystic would tell you, "Hertha thought she was going to the auction to buy another horse, but as soon as she saw me, she fell in love with me, and I have had her heart ever since." I would tell you that just being around Mystic makes my heart expand and puts a smile on my face. Mystic symbolizes my physical body. Almost sixteen hands tall, she is a beautiful Gypsy draft horse with a large, strong body. Even though she is big, she moves with elegance and confidence. She brings her strong, grounded, completely accepting presence to her coaching work.

To the right of Mystic is Captain, a purebred Morgan. He is a dark brown bay with a very refined, beautiful head and exquisitely shaped ears. He is physically strong and moves with elegance. He is very sensitive. Captain's coaching style is to provide kind, loving support and gently nudge his client forward on their path. Captain symbolizes my mental body. Just like me, he sometimes lacks confidence, even though he is strong and capable. To compensate, he pushes himself forward in a way that the other horses and I do not really appreciate. He can be pushy, a not-great leader, and sometimes mean to the other horses. But the more confidence in himself he has, the more he radiates his true inner, sensitive beauty.

Lastly, on the upper right, is Monk, a painted Gypsy cross gelding.

Monk is the Fabio of the horse world—gorgeous and cute at the same time. He does not like short jokes because he is the shortest horse at our ranch, standing at around fourteen hands. He believes he can do anything that any of the taller horses can do. He has a largesse of spirit, heart, and character that is rare. In his coaching, he is very sensitive, gentle, and sweet. Monk symbolizes my spiritual body with his can-do spirit and big motor. There is nothing that Monk cannot do or would not do for me. He is fiery and extremely gentle at the same time.

Monk was the last horse to join my herd. One day I was taking a break at the law office in the middle of a deposition, and I was prompted to check an online horse sale. At first, I tried to deny my prompting because I was in the middle of work. But I checked quickly and saw that this pretty painted Gypsy gelding was selling for less than market value, so I bid on him. I did not think about it for the rest of the day as I returned my focus to work. At the end of the day, I received an email that I was now the proud owner of a Gypsy cross gelding.

Several weeks later, I drove to a place in rural Wyoming that resembled a lunar landscape. I got lost and was a bit frantic by the time I got to the ranch to pick up Monk. As I pulled in, I noticed this horse resembling a pony tied to a hitching rail. I recoiled a bit—had I bought this short of a horse? To make matters worse, he had a respiratory virus and was pretty ill. But while I was examining him, I realized that I was not there to decide whether or not to buy him. He was already mine.

I shifted from critical awareness about what he was not and moved toward getting to know him. He was kind and obedient and jumped right into my trailer. Since then, I have fallen more in love with Monk every day.

But sometimes I continue to misjudge Monk. He is barely taller than the pony classification for horses, and since he still looks like a pony to me sometimes, I expect him to be gentle and a bit lazy. Well, Monk is anything but lazy. When I ride Monk, I experience him as forceful and full of energy. He is strong and kind, but very forward. He is sometimes so ready to just go and cover the country that I wish he would chill a bit. Riding Monk is often not at all restful, and he is hard to contain, even though he is very obedient. Another way of describing Monk is to call him hard-charging, even though he never runs through my reins. It just feels like he is often on the verge of not being controlled. He is not wild, but he is always ready to climb the next hill to see what is on the other side.

I realize that I have lived my life driving forward all the time. Sometimes, I wish I could just slow down my inner drive; it is a fiery compelling energy that keeps me moving to achieve my reason for being, but it is not always pleasant. Maybe riding Monk and learning from him is a path to gaining greater understanding and harmony with my spiritual body. I like to think that my inner spiritual body is majestic, strong, kind, and full of energy like Monk.

There is no longer a separation between my mind and body, my soul and my spirit, the positive and the negative, above and below. All is one. Now, I can embark on utilizing my experience of being reborn into a higher consciousness in service to the light of all oneness—God.

I feel great quietness within. I feel a stillness in all levels of being. I feel the light within me moving when I focus on the light of God. I feel the strength, the power, the love of the light within me. Wholeness is the uniting of all of me with the higher consciousness, the light, and the vibration of God. It took transformation, transmutation, and time for my four lower bodies and my consciousness to discard old habits. Now, after effort, tolerance for pain and discomfort, and courage to open my heart and surrender to the light, I feel the oneness and connection, and it is true and effortless.

At my first coaching retreat, I married my strengths together to be of service to others. I surrendered and trusted myself. I quieted my being, as I had learned to while working with the horses. I fell into being light. No resistance. No trying. No force. Just flowing. I felt one with the light. One with my horses and the women at my retreat. I felt a true partnership with the light in all life.

Oftentimes now, I feel as if I am on the top of the mountain, seeing the sun from a different, higher, closer perspective. Instead of feeling triumphant, I feel humbled to the core of my being because I am in the presence of such light. I look around me and inside me, and I am in awe at God's creation, with which I am now one. Soon, I will descend because once one has climbed the mountain of God, the light is for God to use to illuminate the way for others on their quest for wholeness.

In the book *The Path of the Higher Self*, the Prophets wrote: "Man, know thyself! In order to know himself, man must discover that which is false and that which is true, that which is synthetic and that which is real. Having done this, he can follow the Path that will lead him into all Truth."[31]

While attaining my master's certificate in Gestalt Coaching, I experienced and saw my soul as fractured. I started the process feeling like a five-year-old who could never please her mom, or anyone else. In this portrayal of parts of myself, the five-year-old was kneeling and crouched over herself with her face on the floor. During this process, some of my classmates embodied, or, in other words, were acting as my parts of self. While I experienced and saw this physical portrayal of my unwhole inner being, Melisa asked me how I had accomplished all the things that I had done in my life, if this was my reality. At first, when I answered her, I felt like I was just a hurt little girl who could never get it right. She did not accept my answer as true. Physically, as well as inside my being, I stepped back to review this scenario, and I realized that I had a choice of whether I fell back into this deeply wounded child part of the self or not. I decided then and there that I could raise that part of myself like Jesus raised Lazarus. From that day on, I now know myself differently.

Based on my prior experiences, I realized that for the next twenty-one days, I might still fall back into my old habit patterns. I also realized that if I gently nudged myself out of those patterns and into the reality that at every moment of life, I had the choice of who to be and at what level I wanted to be in vibration. I no longer had to react based on my wounds. Each of the wounds became a portal to greater God-consciousness after I had enough courage to walk into and through the labyrinth of that synthetic consciousness I had created out of avoidance.

My experience of life has changed greatly in this healing journey. I no longer fear what others may think or feel about me. I no longer fear dying. I no longer fear life and the fact that I cannot control what happens around me. I now feel soul freedom to be here now. Mostly, I feel my soul is now free to be me. I finally understand what I read in *The Path of the Higher Self* decades ago: "Individuality is a snowflake etched in fire: it is a singular design. But until the individual discovers the blueprint of his snowflake and just what his singular contribution to the abundant life can be, the true nature of his individuality is not known—the fire in the snowflake remains quiescent."[32]

Wholeness to me equals the soul's divine union with the living God. In many ways, it does not matter which hole, or sense of un-wholeness, an individual has fallen into, for any hole results in us descending into a place that is lower than our divine identity. Each of our paths to wholeness is unique to us and each soul must walk this path individually. This path home is like climbing the highest mountain in the Himalayas. The soul can find sherpas to guide them up the mountain, yet each person's summit is dependent upon their own training in the spiritual, mental, emotional, and physical parts of being. Just as what is needed to climb an actual mountain, soul stamina and tenacity are also very important to reach the summit of being.

I realized in my journey toward wholeness that I had to find a way to bring home my soul fragments that had split apart during the traumas of this human life. My healing journey included invoking light through prayer and my daily spiritual practice, as well as engaging in the hard inner work of resolving ways of being that are not in alignment with my divine identity. My prayers and the intercession of the embodied as well as angels beyond this world assisted me mightily in my quest. I often felt like through love I was wooing my soul to come home inside me. Many times, I had to forgive myself.

I hope to live the rest of my life as a spark to a revolution in which many souls find their path home to wholeness. Being whole is a radical declaration of independence and the greatest act of courage an individual can take. There is no power greater than each of us attaining the greatest light consciousness that we can embody. Mahatma Gandhi, who was a lawyer, is often attributed as saying that we must be the change we wish to see in the world. Our individual embodiment of wholeness, love, harmony, serenity, peace, and light will be the secret super sauce that allows us to create communities in which we love to live.

∞

Epilogue

I often found, during a healing crisis, that I was afraid to feel the pain that I knew was stuck inside me. At one point, I realized that this fear was entwined with my fear of not achieving my dreams. One early morning, my fear of feeling kept me from being able to stay centered in my heart during my early morning prayer and meditation. I asked myself: *Why fear of letting go? Why fear of pain? Why fear of moving forward? Why fear?*

I had heard the teaching that *perfect love casts out all fear*. At that moment, I did not feel perfect love; I felt pain and fear. In an experiment to see if I could get my inner world to move, I decided to go outside to climb the steep hill and search for part of my horse herd. That morning it was very foggy, and the trail and the pasture looked like a place I had never been before. My visibility was limited, and I could not see where the horses might be. I stayed still and searched the hillsides, scanning all the places I usually find them. Even though outer visibility was limited, I started my hike up the path to find the horses. Since I had limited outer vision, I searched my inner intuition to ask for guidance.

As usual, the climb up the hill tested my endurance. When I reached the tree where the horses usually hang out, there were no horses. My intuition pulled me to go south, yet I walked in the other direction so I could check the whole pasture. The mist was thick, and I could not see far. As I was walking the pasture searching for my herd, I realized that it was hunting season for elk and deer. Theoretically, nobody should be hunting in our pasture without permission, and nobody should be shooting on the neighbor's land without a clear line of vision, but the danger was there. I kept going anyway.

I kept scanning the mist to find my herd. At times, I thought I saw horses everywhere I looked, but it was just my mind playing tricks on me out in the mist. Truly, the horses seemed to be nowhere as I searched for them. At one point, I stopped and looked behind me to see if my horses were following me. Nope. Still no horses. I kept searching and moving forward.

During my search, I became lost because of the lowering of the sky with heavy fog. It captured and contained sounds that I usually did not hear when the sky was higher. This made me wonder if it also happened that when the inner fog kept me from seeing, did I also experience more inner noise? When I could not see the heavens clearly, I heard the noises of the earth, closer and louder.

As I stood on the hill searching for the herd, I cried tears of sorrow and great gratitude for the horses that are no longer with me. I realized my attachment, love, and memories of these horses runs very deep. I felt the pain of losing them. I no longer feared the pain because I felt the pain. Those horses were similar to those parts of me that could no longer carry me forward. Just as I grieve and suffer sadness and heart pain because of the horses that are no longer here on Earth with me, I sometimes grieve and suffer sadness when I release parts of myself.

As I was still and surrendering to feeling deep sorrow, the mist suddenly cleared, and the horses I had been searching for appeared. They came trotting toward me. I felt so much joy in joining up with my herd. I led these horses off the high pasture and down to the valley. My outer experience with my horses that day was in some ways similar to my inner healing experience. There were many times on my healing journey when I could not see where I was going. I felt lost. I felt fear. But if I continued moving forward into the mist and discomfort, then I would find an opening and a new awareness that brought me joy.

Another day, instead of eating lunch, I decided I needed to move my body to bring balance to my four lower bodies. I had been working hard and living mostly in my head, so moving my physical body seemed necessary to find balance. So I walked out of the house and up the large hill where my horses roam.

While walking, I called out to Mystic, who usually runs to me. But all my horses headed up the hill and away from me. I felt abandoned, betrayed, frustrated, and a little annoyed. I thought my horses and I were buddies. I wondered, *Why would they leave me?* I decided to not drop into an emotional tirade and instead looked within. I realized I had only given myself an hour to see my horses, which meant I had an agenda. Horses don't really like it when a person has an agenda. Also, I could see the beginnings of shoots of green grass. I knew that when a horse sees, smells, and tastes green grass in the spring, they have a hard time paying attention to anything else.

I would imagine that, to a horse, green grass seems a lot like survival in the way it overrides all their senses. Similarly, when I am in survival mode, I cannot truly hear or tune into my higher consciousness, my four lower bodies, or my inner horses. It seems the green grass and my survival mode block connection.

I pondered my horses leaving me while climbing this long and pretty steep hill covered with sagebrush and punctuated with some gullies and rocks. My focus turned inward, and I thought about how the idea of seeing my horses seemed a lot better in the abstract. Here I was, puffing, climbing this hill, feeling my legs and body work hard. Remember, I was on a schedule, so I had to keep putting one foot in front of the other. I realized that my inner climb to wholeness also often seemed better in the abstract than in the actual experience of climbing. It is hard work.

Finally, I summited over the top and saw the horses still in the distance. Even though I had not yet reached them, I had already found my reward. My view of the world changed up there. I could see the horizon go on forever and storms in the distance. I could smell the life and freshness of spring. Soon, I reached the horses and connected with each one. I did not have as much time as I would have liked because of my deadline. Also, there was weather moving in.

On the way down the hill, I realized that the descent was more dangerous than the ascent. It is steep, and any misstep could result in a sprained ankle, knee injury, or broken bones. I was assaulted by a mixture of rain, snow, sleet, and hail that hurt my cheeks. Now, even though I was on the descent, I was not so sure of my decision to leave the comfort of my house to go climbing to see my horses.

My outer climb, weather and all, was very similar to my experiences with inner climbing toward wholeness. I had to exert energy and carefully plant each foot to determine the safest way both up and down the hill. Once I was in the experience of climbing to my horses, for a moment, I wished I had stayed back where I was warm and comfortable. Then my view opened to the heavens and all of me changed because I made it to the top. In my experience, I have always found the trek up the mountain to the inner summit of being worth the effort, struggle, pain, and inconvenience.

When I reached the inner mountaintop, I felt great quietness within. I felt stillness at all levels of being. I felt the light within me. I felt strength, love, and awareness beyond my normal human understanding. I began to know that wholeness is the union with the higher mind, and it is available for all who pursue truth and withstand the winds of healing transformation. I understood that the purpose of wholeness is to become someone who shows the way to others who are also seeking divine wholeness.

My Prayer

Dear Father/Mother, God of Light, Love, and Divine oneness,

In the name of my mighty I AM presence, I pray for the infusion of God's light, love, and wholeness into every part of my being; into every wrinkle of my consciousness, known or unknown to my outer mind; into every cell and atom of my physical manifestation.

I pray for the oneness of the Buddha and the Mother, in figure eight flow of Alpha and Omega, to fill my consciousness and form with the unity of Divine consciousness.

I pray for the light moving within every aspect of my being to move upward into my outer consciousness, to all that is not light. As this healing process fills in me, I pray for strength, awareness, and awakening that I may choose to identify with wholeness rather than those worn-out aspects of my identity I have created through many lives because I have forgotten who I AM in my Divine identity.

I pray for the grace of awareness and memory of my Divine identity so that as the light within me increases and this fiery furnace of light and fire in my heart acts as a magnet to draw in those fragments of self that I have discarded around the universe, I may keep my vision on my true self while these parts come home.

I pray for grace, Divine light, and love to hold me together as I sort through the symphonies of self to determine that which is real and that which is not.

I pray that my eye be single, my heart strong, and my mind quiet as I feel the great discomfort of the transmutational total healing of my soul toward total oneness with Divine light.

I pray that my heart and being may be infused with the grace of Divine courage to keep me on the path toward wholeness even when the trek upward feels too hard.

I pray that my human and spiritual heart be awakened and infused with Divine love and the patterns of true harmony so that I may hold the balance for my own and others' transformational healing and coming home to true Divine self.

I pray that my soul be cradled in the cosmic egg and that I will be reborn into the outer manifestation fully integrated into my physical body of my original Divine blueprint and geometrical design as created by God.

I pray that my eyes see the beauty of light in all creation.

I pray that every ounce of wholeness that I gain be placed on the altar of healing for Mother Earth and all life thereon.

I pray that the light within me be a spark that grows into a revolution for wholeness so that all life finds the path home to oneness with the Divine.

I pray that my heart and the light and love therein create a super-highway from Earth to the heavens so that all who so choose can find their path to wholeness.

MY PRAYER

I pray for Divine guidance every second of this day so that I may be in the right place at the right time at all levels of being.

I pray for Divine love and light so that at every second of this day I may be in the right vibration, balance, and harmony to dispense God's light and love through my body temple for the blessing of all life on Earth.

Oh Lord, Father/Mother God, let this prayer in my heart be magnified and multiplied by your holy angels and all beings that reside in the higher realms so that many on Earth will receive the greatest blessing possible this day for the awakening of their path home to wholeness and oneness with their Divine identity, as they were originally created by God.

All my love,
Hertha Louise Lund

Acknowledgments

My parents, Robert and Jeanne Lund, gave me the best upbringing they knew how. They worked hard to raise me and my brothers and sisters on ranches in Montana. Ranch life shaped my soul and I learned to soak in strength, self-reliance, and belief in the beauty of nature to shine forth God's blessings.

Without meeting Elizabeth Clare Prophet and studying the teachings published by the Summit Lighthouse, I would not have had enough fire in my heart to persevere and find the courage and love to embody divine wholeness. By God's grace, I was gifted with the assistance of Dr. Kellyn Milani, ND; Lauren Oeschsli, LAC; Dr. Amy Haynes, ND; Dr. Alisun Bonville, ND; Dr. Kimberly Maxwell, DC; and Heidi Soper, body-soul practitioner on my healing journey. Also, I was blessed with the loving care of Dr. Donna Lidren, PhD; Lucile Yaney, LCSW; and Melisa Pearce, Gestaltist and psychotherapist.

Working with Donna Galassi, my publishing consultant at KN Literary Arts, as well as with Sarah Bossenbroek was a slice of heaven on Earth as we collaborated to bring my book into fruition. Also, Elina Vaysbeyn, Elisabeth Rinaldi, Christina Thiele, and Audra Figgins have all been wonderful to work with, and I am so grateful they shared their immense publishing talents to assist me.

The love of my husband, John A. Grande, carried me through some very tough spots in my healing journey. I am grateful to have found him and to share our life journeys together.

Lastly, I thank God and horses for carrying me when I could no longer continue on my own. Without my relationships with God and horses, this book would not have been possible.

Endnotes

1. Mark L. Prophet and Elizabeth Clare Prophet, *The Path of the Higher Self*, Climb the Highest Mountain Series, (Corwin Springs, Montana: Summit University Press, 1986), xv–xvi, quoted with permission from Summit University Press.

2. Malcolm Gladwell, *Outliers: The Story of Success*, (New York: Little, Brown and Company, 2008).

3. Kelly McDaniel, *Mother Hunger: How Adult Daughters Can Understand and Heal from Lost Nurturance, Protection, and Guidance*, (Carlsbad, California: Hay House, 2021), 6.

4. Ibid., 113.

5. Saint John of the Cross, "Dark Night of the Soul," trans. Edgar Allison Peers (1953), this work is in the public domain.

6. Melisa Pearce, *What the Heck Is Gestalt?*, (Elizabeth, Colorado: Touched By A Horse, Inc, 2019), 22.

7. McDaniel, *Mother Hunger*, 139.

8. John Welwood, *Toward a Psychology of Awakening: Buddhism, Psychotherapy, and the Path of Personal and Spiritual Transformation*, (Boulder, Colorado: Shambhala Publications, 2000), 19.

9. Ibid., 15.

10. Jack Kornfield, *A Path with Heart: A Guide Through the Perils and Promises of Spiritual Life*, (New York: Bantam Books, 1993), 168.

11. Kristin Neff, *Self Compassion: The Proven Power of Being Kind to Yourself*, (New York: HarperCollins, 2011), 5, Kindle edition.

12. Nisargadatta Maharaj, *I Am That*, (Durham, North Carolina: The Acorn Press, 2005), 70.

13. Welwood, *Toward a Psychology of Awakening*, 19.

14. Ibid.

15. Judith Blackstone, *The Enlightenment Process: A Guide to Embodied Spiritual Awakening*, (St. Paul, Minnesota: Paragon House, 2008), 66.

16. Michael Singer, *Living Untethered: Beyond the Human Predicament*, (Oakland, California: New Harbinger Publications, 2022), 181.

17. Heidi Soper, "Body and Mind Therapy Studio," June 5, 2023, Bodyandmindtherapystudio.com, June 5, 2023.

18. Bonnie Greenwell, *Energies of Transformation: A Guide to the Kundalini Process*, (Saratoga, California: Shakti River Press, 1988).

19. Ibid, 9–10.

20. Ibid, 1–2.

21. Prophet and Prophet, *The Path of the Higher Self*, 331.

22. Welwood, *Toward a Psychology of Awakening*, 5.

23. Ibid, 107.

24. Brené Brown, *Rising Strong: How the Ability to Reset Transforms the Way We Live, Love, Parent, and Lead*, (New York: Random House, 2017), 50.

25. Bessel van der Kolk, *The Body Keeps the Score: Brain, Mind, and Body in the Healing of Trauma*, (New York: Penguin Books, 2014).

26. Brown, *Rising Strong*, 113.

27. McDaniel, *Mother Hunger*, 140.

28. Ibid.

29. Mark L. Prophet and Elizabeth Clare Prophet, *Saint Germain on Alchemy: Formulas for Self-Transformation*, (Corwin Springs, Montana: Summit University Press, 1993), 21.

30. Ibid, 6.

31. Prophet and Prophet, *The Path of the Higher Self*, xxv.

32. Prophet and Prophet, *The Path of the Higher Self*, 147.

About the Author

Hertha Lund is a lifelong lover of horses and the founder of Four Horses for Wholeness retreat center in central Montana. Her path to her passion and life work as a writer and healer partnering with horses has been circuitous. During college, she studied pre-medicine both for humans and horses and then transitioned to study journalism. After covering Congress and the United States Supreme Court as a journalist, she went to law school. She founded her own law firm, Lund Law, and has served landowners to protect their private property and water rights since 1995.

A near-death experience changed her life, and she sought assistance to heal and studied Equine Gestalt Coaching. Now, in addition to running her law practice, she offers individual, group, and retreat coaching on the Grande family ranch. Hertha is also a professional public speaker and loves sharing her life experiences regarding healing and wholeness with others.

About Four Horses for Wholeness

Specializing in serving those who are searching for meaning in life, who want to experience transformational healing, and who believe that horses can help us heal, Four Horses for Wholeness offers retreats in rural Montana, as well as individual and group coaching and online coaching. During the summer months, we offer two retreats per month where visitors can unplug, experience peace in nature, and allow horses to help them find their authentic, true selves.

Find out more at fourhorsesforwholeness.com, or on the Four Horses for Wholeness Facebook and Instagram (@fourhorsesforwholeness). Call us at 406-282-4002. Email 4Horses4Wholeness@gmail.com to sign up for our quarterly newsletter.